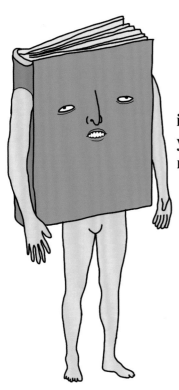

if you read me
you will feel
more positive

D1214876

i am so depressed

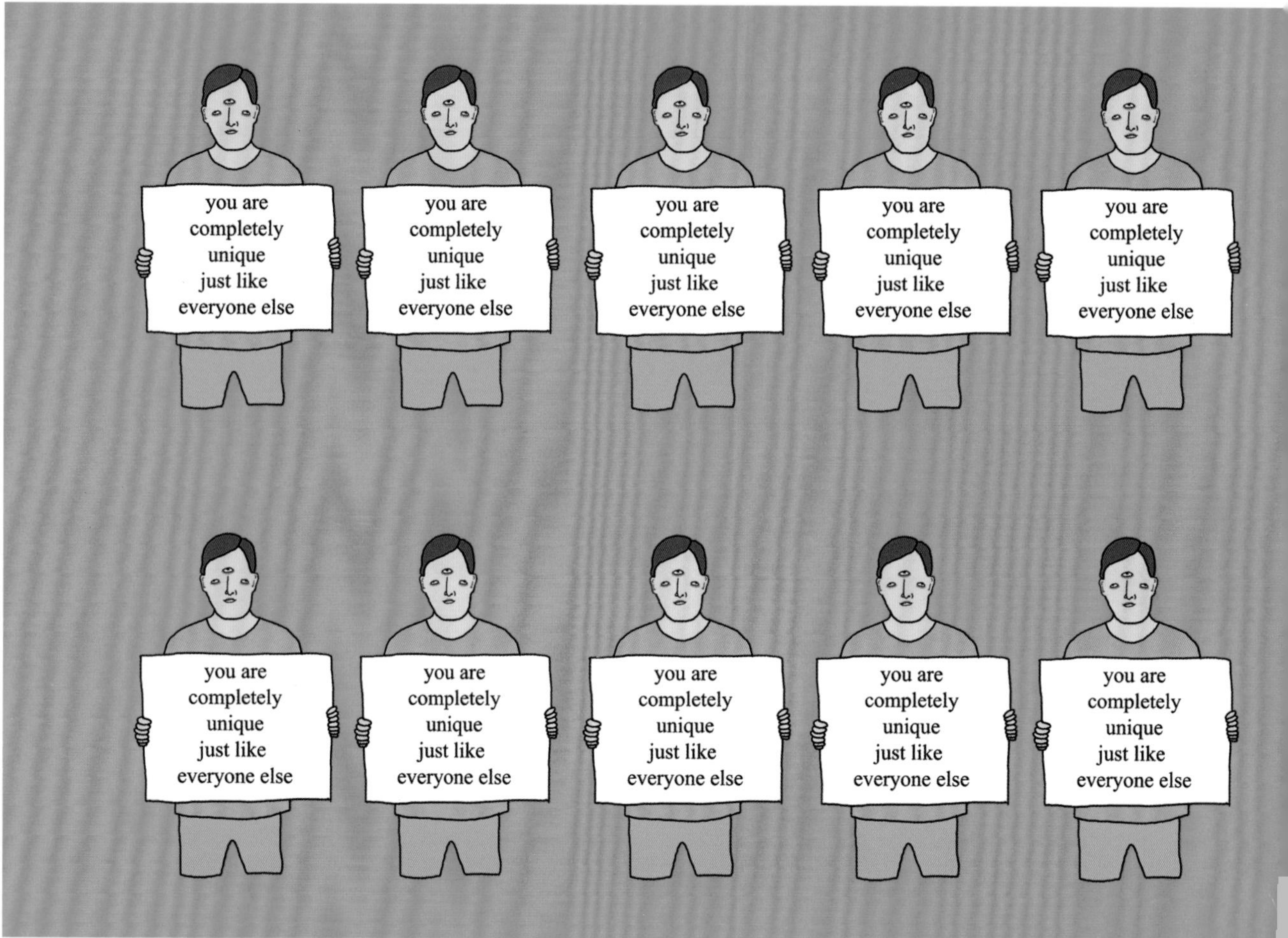
you are completely unique just like everyone else
you are completely unique just like everyone else
you are completely unique just like everyone else
you are completely unique just like everyone else
you are completely unique just like everyone else
you are completely unique just like everyone else
you are completely unique just like everyone else
you are completely unique just like everyone else
you are completely unique just like everyone else
you are completely unique just like everyone else

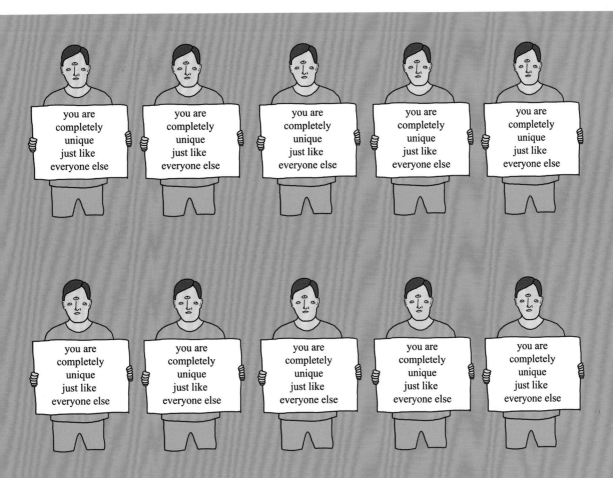

this book is dedicated to all of my friends
and my mum

# Motivational Quotes to Help You Be More Positive

chris (simpsons artist)

First published in Great Britain in 2015 by Trapeze
This paperback edition first published in Great Britain in 2018 by Trapeze
an imprint of The Orion Publishing Group Ltd
Carmelite House, 50 Victoria Embankment
London EC4Y 0DZ

An Hachette UK Company

1 3 5 7 9 10 8 6 4 2

A CIP catalogue record for this book is
available from the British Library.

ISBN (Paperback) 978 1 4091 8184 2

Printed in Italy

www.orionbooks.co.uk

MIX
Paper from
responsible sources
FSC® C015829

## introduction

if you wake up in the morning time
and you dont like what you have become

then it is up to you to change yourself
and become the person who you truly wish to be

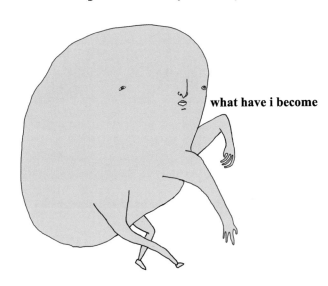

**what have i become**

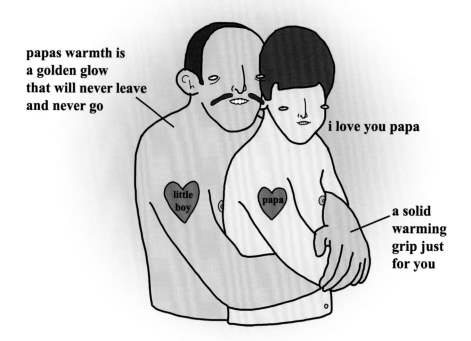

papas warmth is
a golden glow
that will never leave
and never go

i love you papa

little
boy

papa

a solid
warming
grip just
for you

a fathers love will always
keep you warm

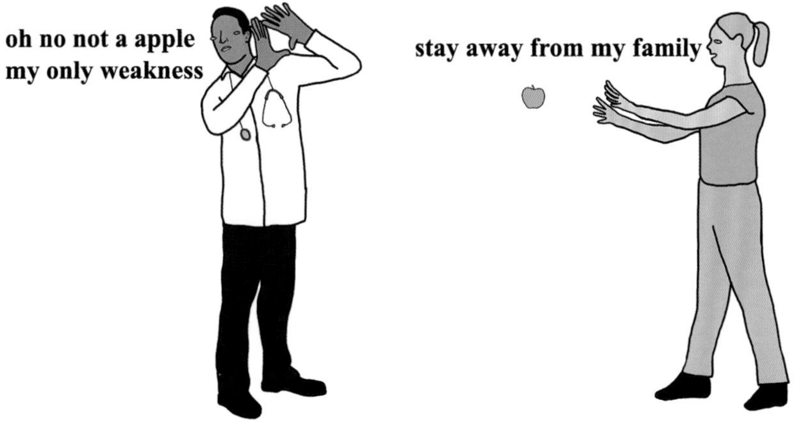
oh no not a apple
my only weakness
stay away from my family

a apple a day keeps the doctor away

just close your eyes
i will do all the work
ok

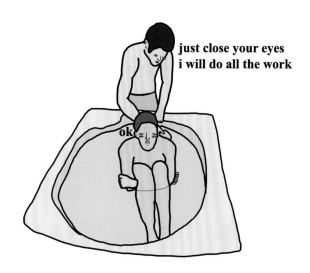

washing a mans back will make yourself feel like
you are good at something for once in your life

# be happy while you are living

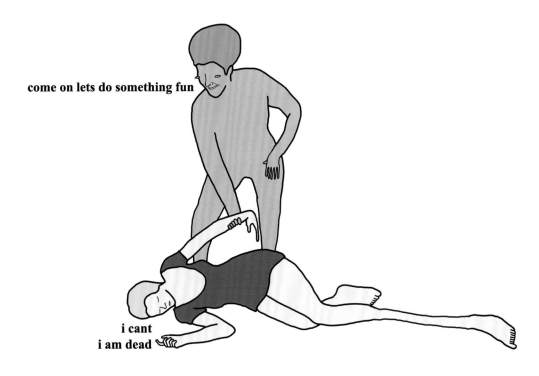

come on lets do something fun

i cant
i am dead

# because it is almost impossible to do when you are dead

everyone is looking for something
maybe it is you

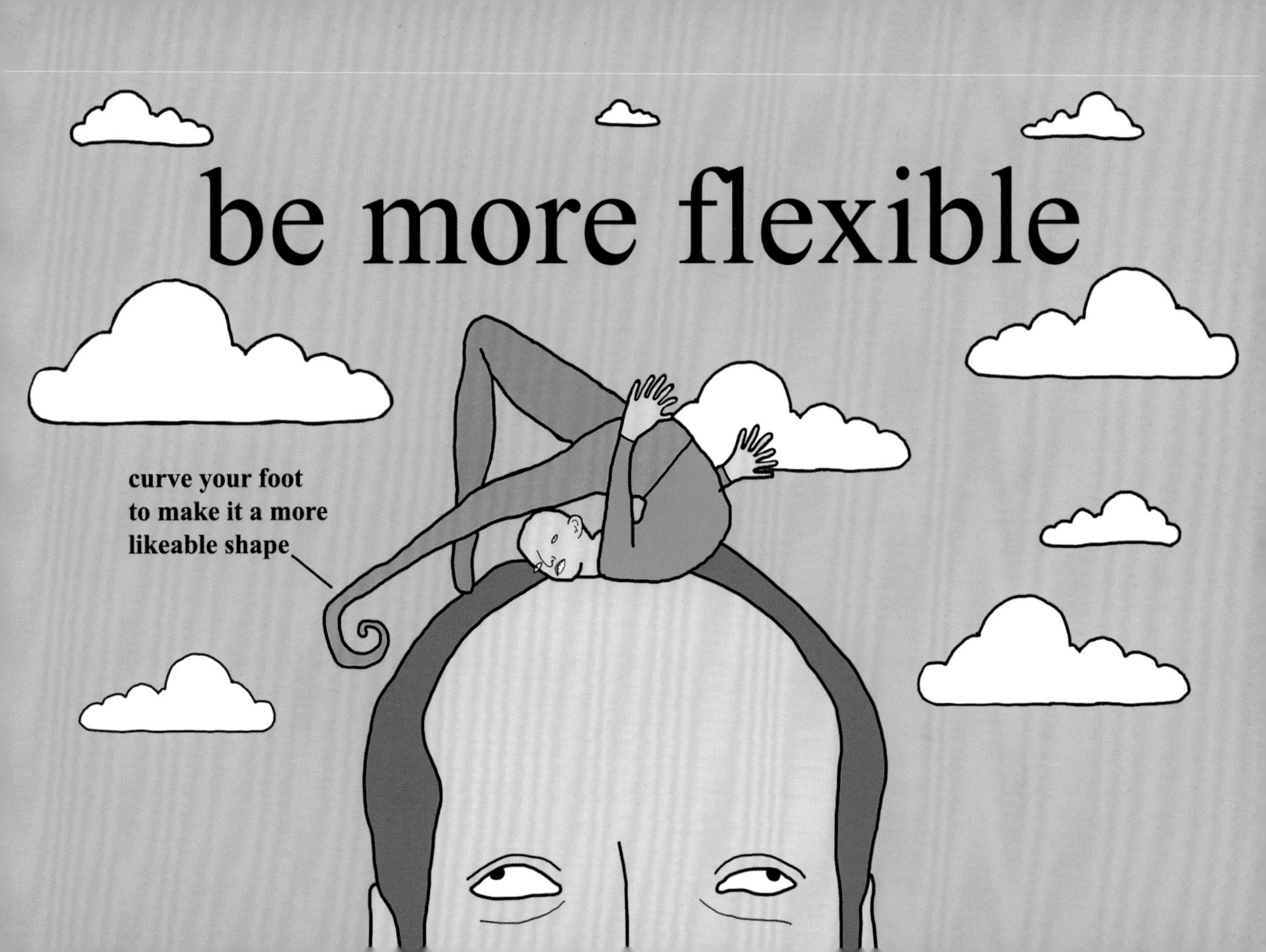
be more flexible
curve your foot
to make it a more
likeable shape

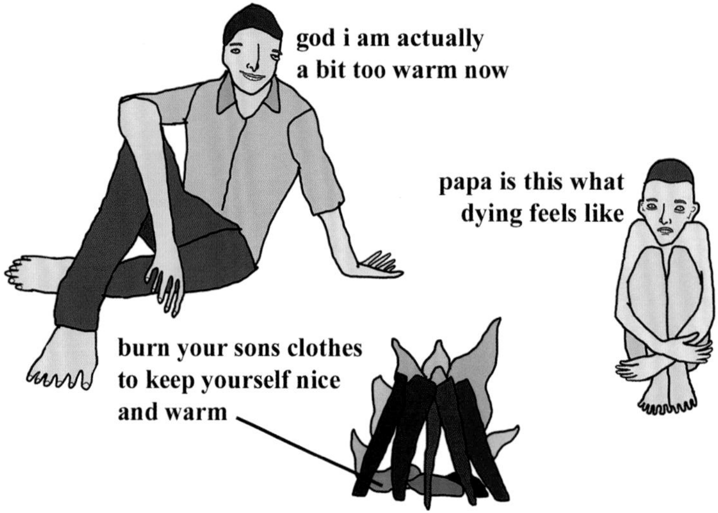
god i am actually
a bit too warm now
papa is this what
dying feels like
burn your sons clothes
to keep yourself nice
and warm

nothing says i love you
more than the warm breeze of a fire burning
underneath a blanket of stars

trust me it only hurts
for about a second
i am so worried

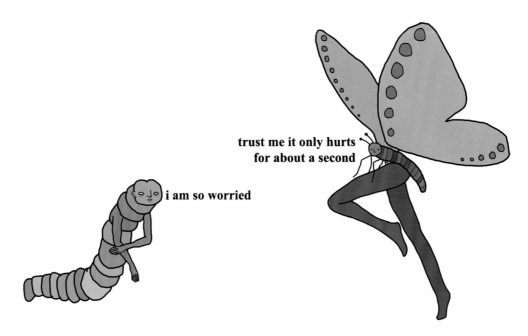

it is important for people to try new things
because if you dont try new things then you might not
become a butterfly at the end of it and if you dont try
anything new then you might just be a caterpillar
for the rest of your life

his collection is complete

this one reminds him to smile

# collect feathers
# to keep yourself positive

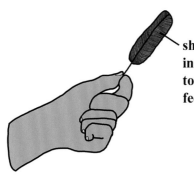

she will keep this one in her bag so she can touch it when she feels depressed

maybe things arent so bad after all

he is crying because he has found a photograph of his wife sharpening a pencil for his son on his first day of school

eye spit

it is ok to cry sometimes because tears are just sad spit that comes out of your eyes

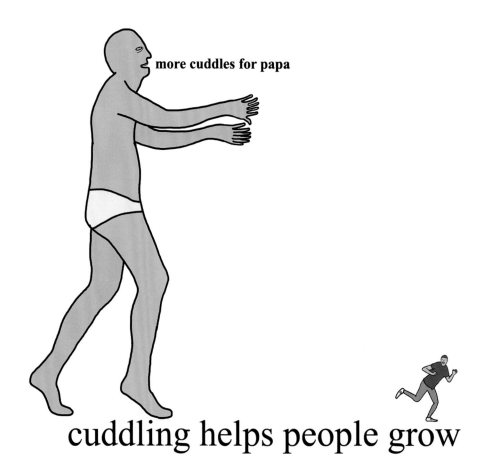

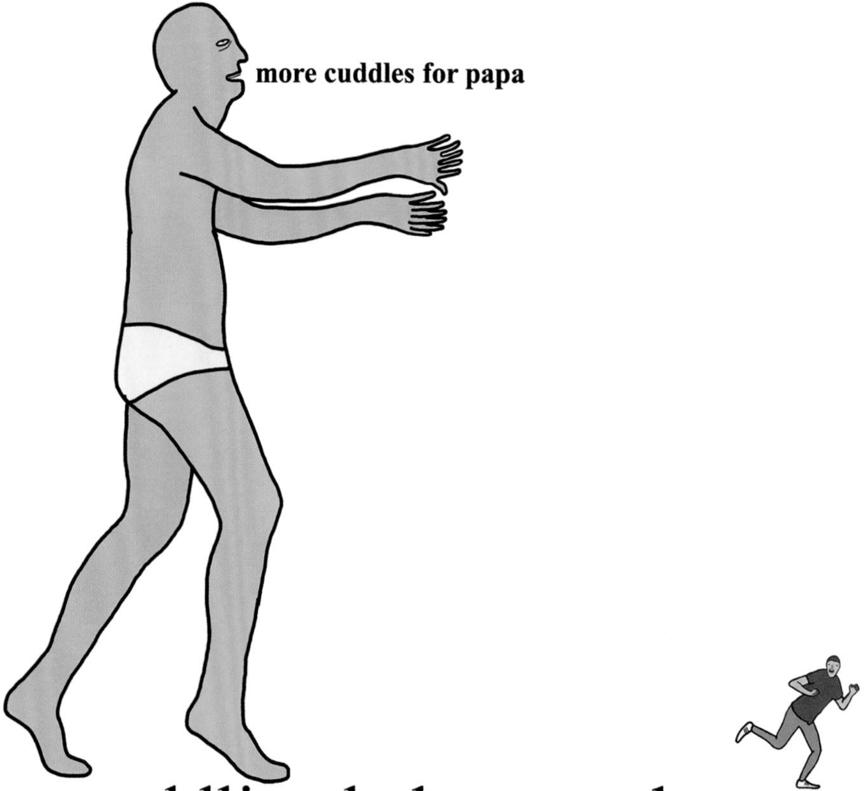
more cuddles for papa

cuddling helps people grow

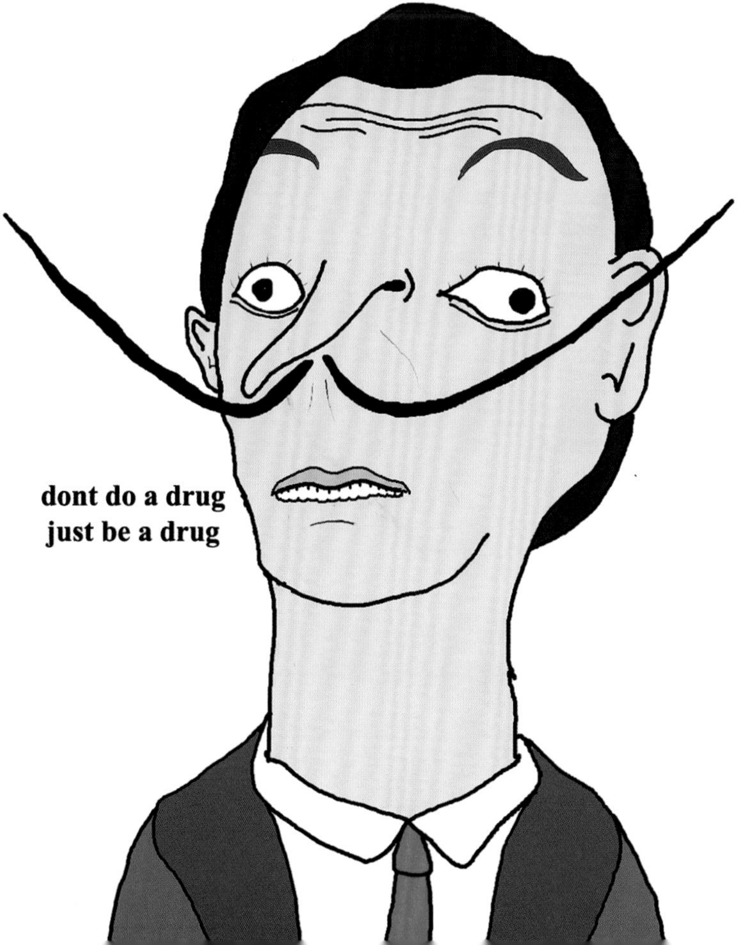
dont do a drug
just be a drug

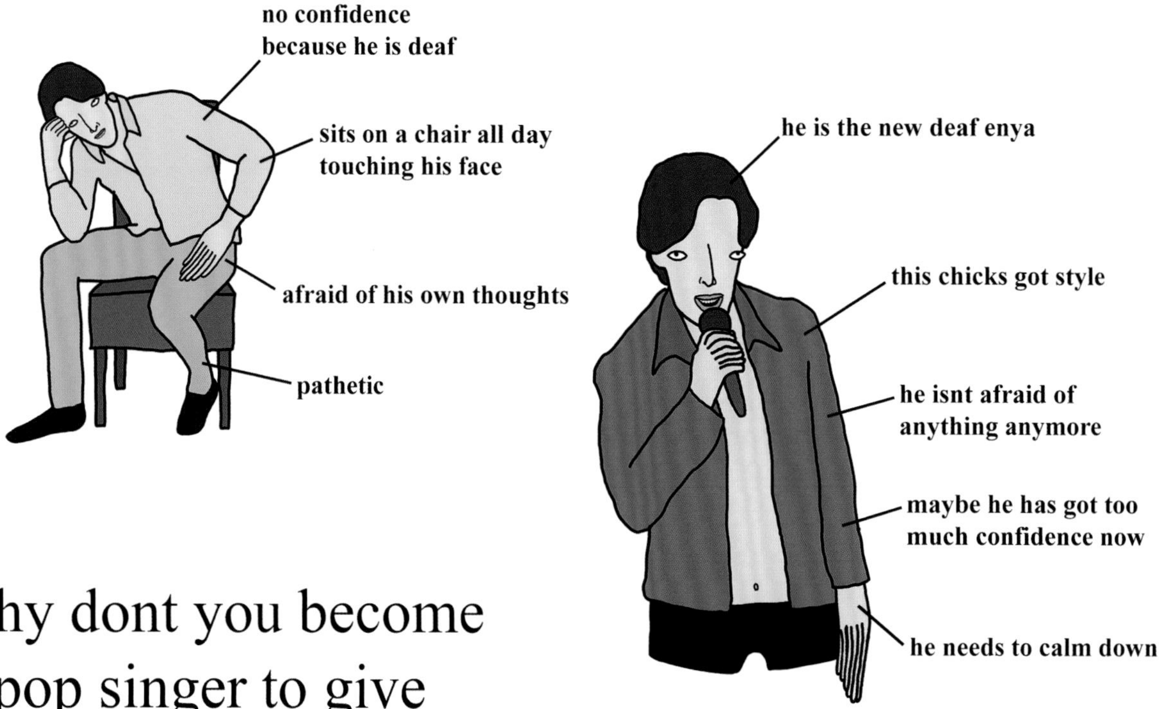
no confidence
because he is deaf
sits on a chair all day
touching his face
afraid of his own thoughts
pathetic
he is the new deaf enya
this chicks got style
he isnt afraid of
anything anymore
maybe he has got too
much confidence now
he needs to calm down

why dont you become
a pop singer to give
yourself a bit of confidence

she thinks her
kettle was cursed
by a witch
oh god
she is frightened that her
arm will fall off if she
makes a cup of tea

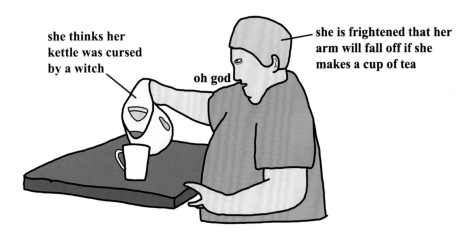

do the things that you fear most
because they probably arent as
scary as you think they are
inside of your head

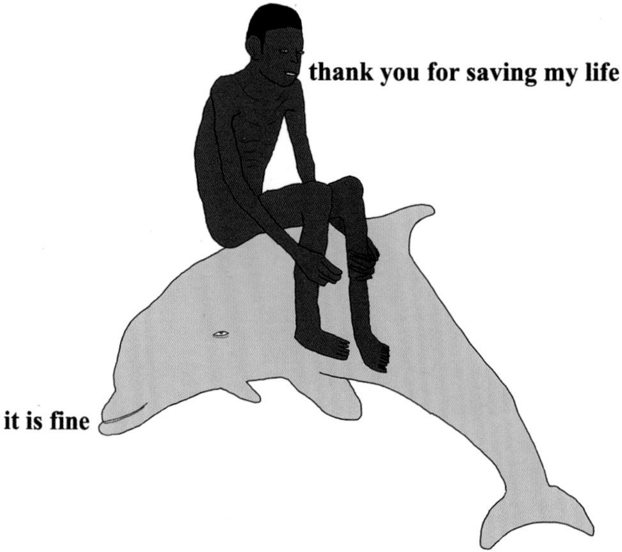
thank you for saving my life
it is fine

a true friend is someone who will rescue you from a drought
without even thinking about their own safety

dont have favourites

because everyone has favourites

and if you have favourites then you are the same as everyone else

and if you are the same as everyone else then you wont be anybodys favourite

jesus christ
he is massive

he is so large

600 years ago today on a cold north pole night something magical happened under a star that shined so bright that is right it is the birth of our lord saviour baby jesus christ. a lot of people sometimes always forget the true story of christmas time so pull up a seat or borrow a stool from a friend and listen to the tale of the newborn king. when mary was lay in her bedroom on christmas eve feeling really excited for it being christmas day a angel whos name is called gabron floated down from heaven to tell her that while she was sleeping the other night santa claus laid an egg inside of her and mary said i cant believe it and then gabron did a massive screaming laugh that sounded like someone rolling a barrel of children off a roof and he said well we will see about that haha and then he tapped his finger on his nose 3 times and he did a slow motion wink and then he completely vanished into a puff of steam and then mary ran over to her boyfriend josephs house and she told him that santa claus had laid an egg inside of her and joseph said he couldnt believe it and mary said i know it is the one thing i least expected to happen and then suddenly a bright star whos name is called north appeared

in the sky above them and he told them to follow him quickly before it is too late so mary and joseph climbed onto a donkeys back and they galloped after the star which led them to a barn in the middle of the north pole and he said this is where you are going to have your baby and mary said are you actually kidding me this place is so disgusting and it stinks of camels and the star said i know but it is the best i could do at this short notice and joseph said fair enough this will do i suppose and he looked at mary and rolled his eyes and then the star said good and it disappeared into the darkness and then 3 wise men came to the barn because they heard there was some sort of birthing going to be happening and joseph said they could watch if they each give mary a gift so they gave mary some gold earrings a 6 pack of frankfurter sausages and a olly murs cd because those are the things that she enjoys the most and then as quickly as a christmas wish mary starts pooing the egg out of her bum and one of the 3 wise men bursts out laughing when he sees the top of the egg coming out of marys bum and his laughing makes the other wise men burst out laughing as well and joseph kept on looking at them and tutting and then he said either you three just shut up or just stand outside of the barn because you are putting my mary off laying her egg and then mary did one last thick deep push and the egg completely slid out of her bum and landed on the barn floor and cracked open and baby jesus slowly climbed out of the egg and when joseph sees jesus he cant believe how big he is and he screams jesus christ he is massive and that is why they decided to call him jesus christ because it is what everyone always says when they first see the size of him and as mary and joseph and baby jesus and the three wise men all lay in the barn cuddling each others legs they hear the sound of sleigh bells high above their heads and at that very moment they knew that the spirit of christmas will forever live on inside of each and every single one of us for as long as baby jesus name is remembered and that is why on christmas eve santa claus lays an egg down everyones chimneys so they will always be reminded of that magical night when mary laid our lord saviour baby jesus christ out of her bum and into our hearts.

suck your stomach
in and out really
quickly to locate
your air sacks if
you cant find them

listen to your air sacks
like you are having a
listen to the sound of
your mums sack
when you was inside
of her when you was
a little boy

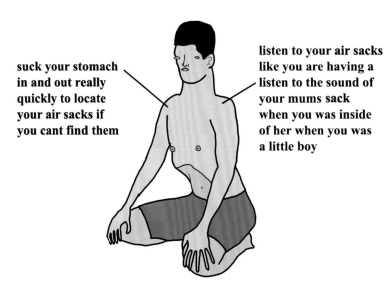

dont forget to breathe

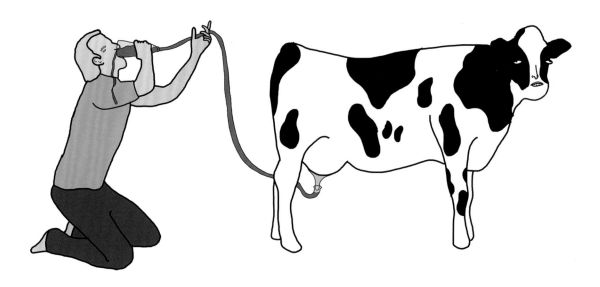

try and drink a smaller
amount of meat

delicious wet soup

eating soup in the rain is like eating
a sandwich that grows with every bite

it doesnt matter what type of shape
you are because all that really matters
is what type of shape your eyes make
when he tells you that he loves you

every
shadow
is a friend

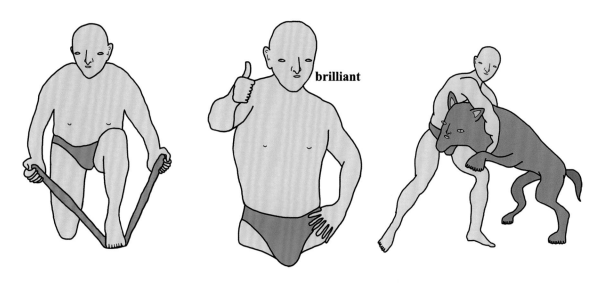

brilliant

exercising will help you
live for longer and it will also help
you build up strength to finally capture
the wolf that killed your wife

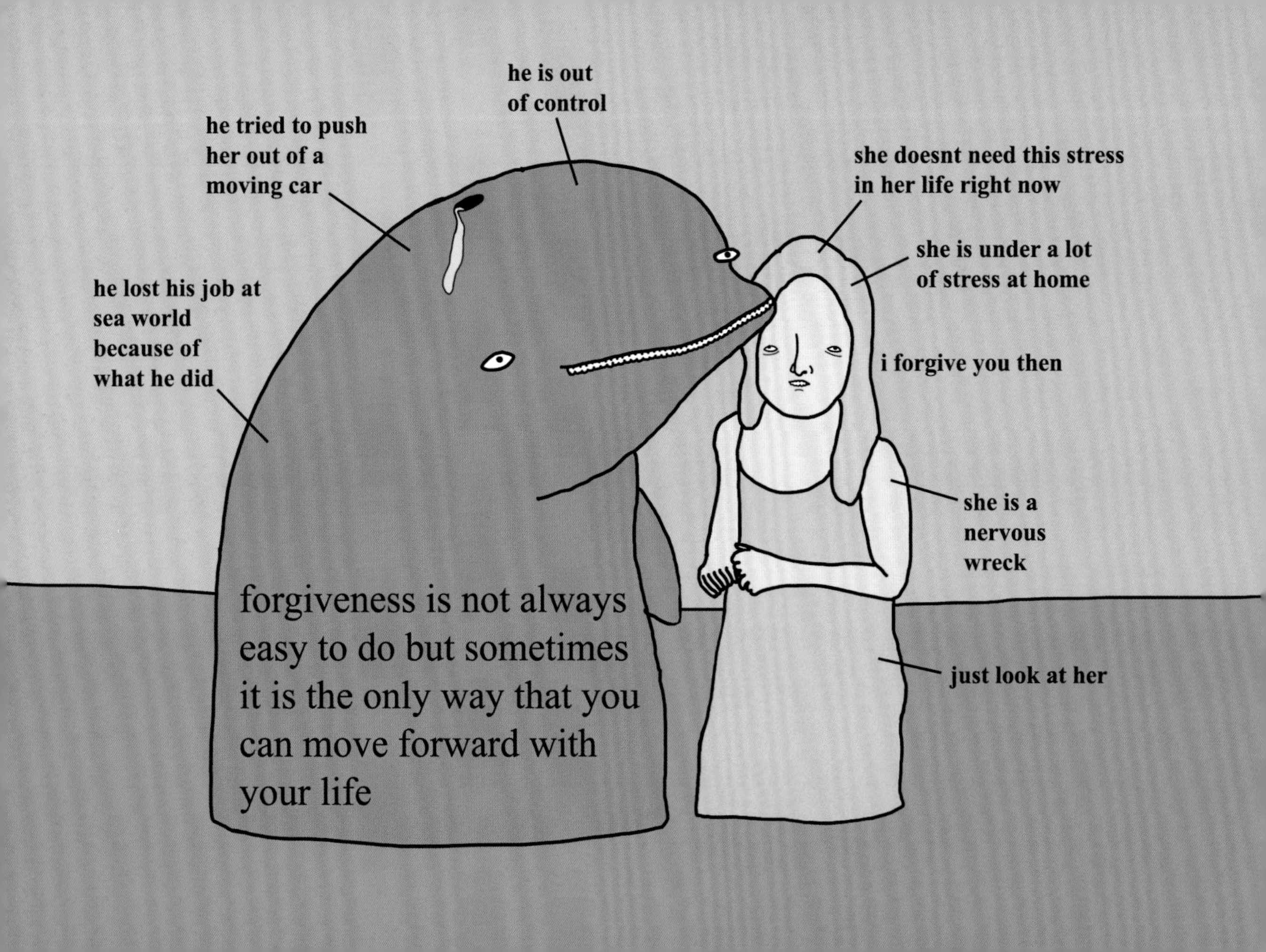
he is out
of control
he tried to push
her out of a
moving car
she doesnt need this stress
in her life right now
she is under a lot
of stress at home
he lost his job at
sea world
because of
what he did
i forgive you then
she is a
nervous
wreck
forgiveness is not always easy to do but sometimes it is the only way that you can move forward with your life
just look at her

dont eat wool

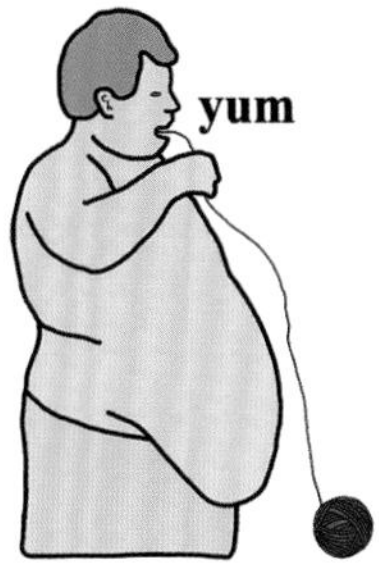
yum

it will just clog up your stomach

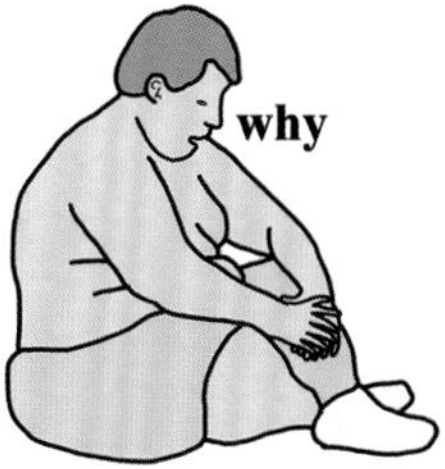
why

and you will die

i dont care what you say
i am wearing it
i am nearly 29

if you want to make outfits out of bits of cloth
that you found in your loft then you should
just do it because you are a grown man
and it is your body not your mums

butterflys dont taste of butter
they just taste of flys

he is selfish

the butterfly has been a family
pet for 15 and a half years

he wanted the buttery
taste inside of himself

everyone in his family wishes
the butterfly ate him instead

never be sad
because somewhere there is someone
who is falling in love with your smile

brian you look
absolutely great

thanks i feel
absolutely great
haha

wear some gold lipstick to
make yourself look and feel great

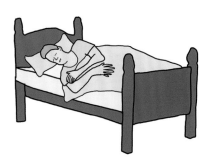

gold isnt the most important thing in your life
the most important thing in your life is
your family and your friends and your wife
and i think that it is better for a person to live their life happily
in a wooden bed and be remembered than it is to spend their life
feeling sad and be buried in a golden coffin and be forgotten

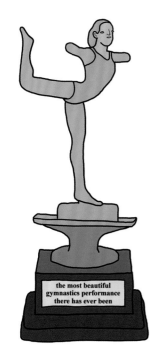

the most beautiful
gymnastics performance
there has ever been

dont think about all of the
things in your life that you cant
do for yourself just think about all of the
things in your life that you can achieve
if you just start believing in yourself

make me feel young again

i love it

a new hairstyle is a great way to make yourself feel young again

happiness is different for everyone

some people like eating ham

the ham gives
him a powerful
feeling that he
cant control

and some people like putting ham
on their face and pretending to
be a killer from a film

keep the change
you filthy idiot

it is everyones favourite family christmas film about child neglect and torture that is right it is home alone. i have done a picture of the main character from home alone and his name is called kevin but everyone just calls him kev the slev because he is always making spit go down his chin to make people laugh and if you havent seen home alone before then you should have a watch of it tonight or tomorrow night because it is really good and my best bit in it is when kevin pours a can of coke on to his pizza and he says to his mum to clean it up and then his mum says ugh kevin you are such a disease and then she locks him in the loft and his cousin wees on him when he is sleeping and then his family all decide to go on holiday and they leave kevin in the loft on his own because he is the most unpopular one in his family and when he wakes up in the morning time he realises that everyone is gone and he goes in to his mum and dads bedroom and he stares at himself in the mirror for ages and he keeps on saying why and then he sees 2 robbers outside of his house and he hears them saying that they are going to rob his house at 9 o clock on the dot and kevin says yeah right are you hell going to have a rob of my house you homeless idiots so he sets up loads of some traps in his house so that he can kill the robbers and then when it is night time he trys to make himself something to eat but all that he can find in the cupboards is plastic so he has to eat plastic for his christmas dinner and it made me feel really sorry for him because he was nearly crying because it was so sharp and it was cutting his throat when he is swallowing it and he kept on saying so sharp and then he hears the robbers trying to get in to his house so he goes in to the kitchen and he says to the robbers that if they come in to his house he will kill them and the robbers just start laughing and they say ha ha you cant kill us you are only 5 years old and we are both 20 years old and then kevin says ok then you asked for it and he puts a flame thrower with a knife on the end of it out of the door and he flames them and he slashes their legs with the knife as well and the robbers have to put their faces in to the snow to cool themselfs and then the tall robber stands on a nail and it goes right inside of his foot and it is so disgusting and a massive spider comes out of his mouth because he is screaming so much and then when the robbers are lay on the floor kevin goes up to them and he starts laughing and he makes loads of spit go down his chin and he says you messed with the wrong 5 year old and then the police come and they arrest the robbers and kevin says that was close and then he goes to sleep because he is so tired and starved and when he wakes up in the morning time he goes downstairs and he stands in his living room and he looks at a picture of himself for about a hour and then he hears some footsteps behind him and he says i know them familiar footsteps and he turns around and it is his mum and she says merry christmas kevin and he says merry christmas mum and she realises that she does like him after all and then right at the end kevins dad finds a gold tooth on the floor and he says to kevin did you loose your gold tooth and kevin says oh yeah i wondered where that thing went to and he puts his gold tooth back inside of his mouth and then there is a close up of kevins face and it goes in slow motion and he says merry christmas in a really deep voice and then the film just ends and it really is the best christmas film that there has ever been.

having a walk next to a friend
in the darkness of night is better
than having a walk on your own
in the lightness of day

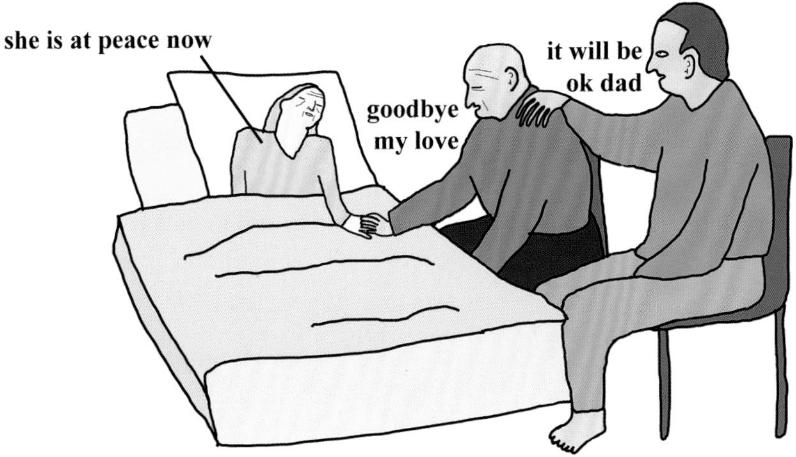
she is at peace now
goodbye my love
it will be ok dad

it is better to say goodbye in peace
than to say hello in pain

he eats plastic bags
i dont want my family
to see me like this
he has been sleeping
at the bottom of the garden
under a bit of wood he found
at the back of the shop
he thinks he has let his family down
he wishes he could
turn back the clock
his son thinks he is a fireman
he is a bag of meat

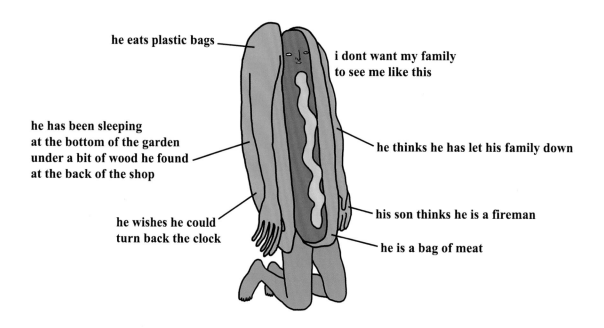

talk to your family about how you feel
they wont be angry at you forever

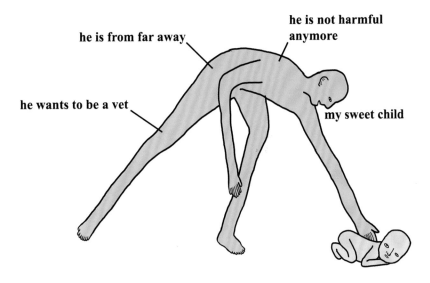

he is from far away

he is not harmful anymore

he wants to be a vet

my sweet child

if you see it then it can be yours
so just go over to it and pick it up

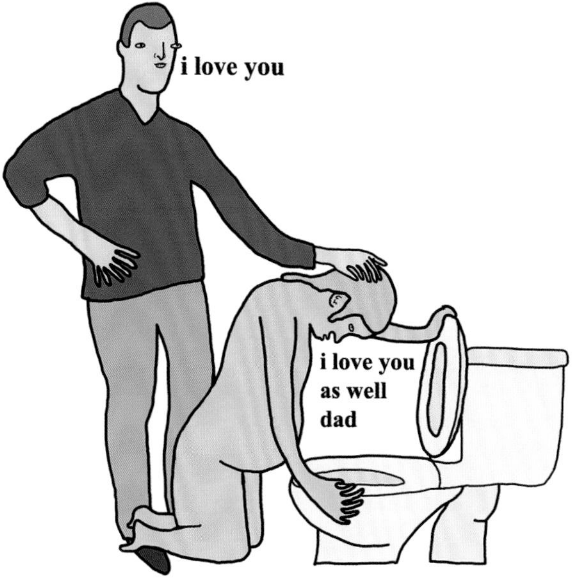
i love you
i love you as well dad

if you feel sick just be sick
if you love someone just tell them

# if you love something never let it go

if you love something so much then you
should never let it go because it is the most
tiniest of things in your life that make the
most biggest difference and sometimes you
dont even realise it was even
there until it is gone

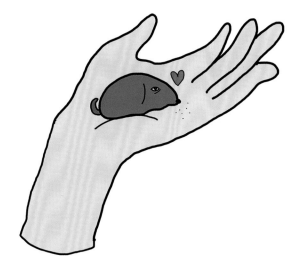

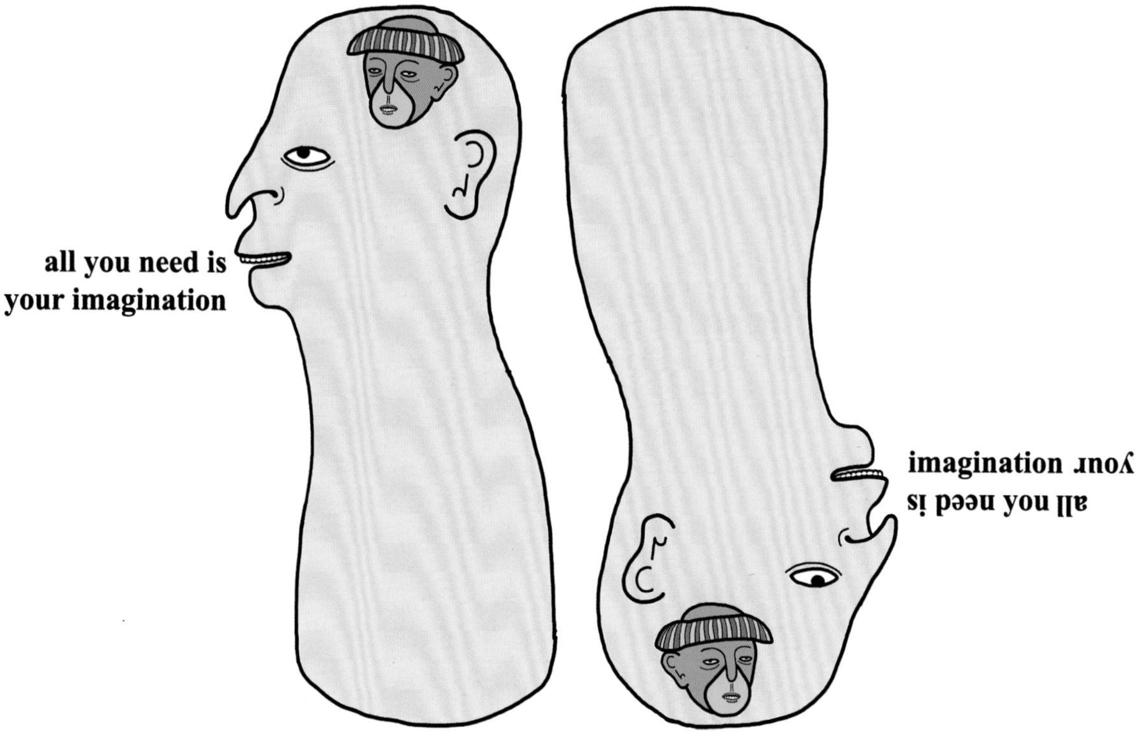

all you need is
your imagination
all you need is
your imagination

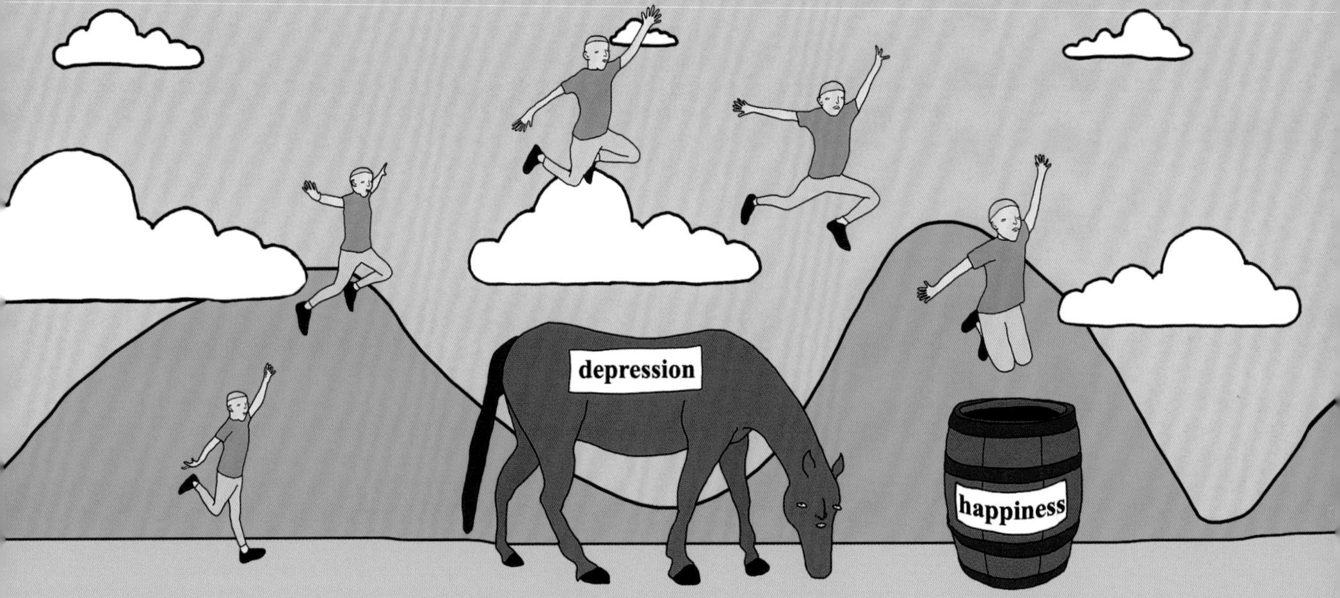
depression
happiness

jump over depression like you are
jumping over a massive brown horse
into barrel of happiness

# it is fine to miss someone

because it just means you remember
all of the beautiful things about them

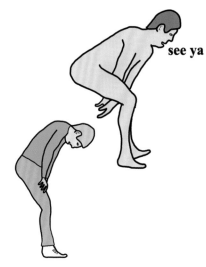

you can do it
just go for it
jump over a little boys head

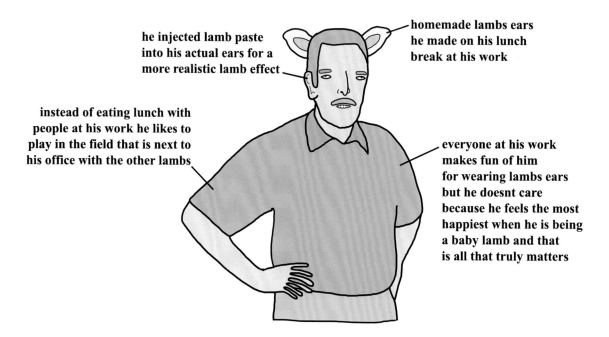

he injected lamb paste into his actual ears for a more realistic lamb effect

homemade lambs ears he made on his lunch break at his work

instead of eating lunch with people at his work he likes to play in the field that is next to his office with the other lambs

everyone at his work makes fun of him for wearing lambs ears but he doesnt care because he feels the most happiest when he is being a baby lamb and that is all that truly matters

if you want to be a baby lamb then just be a baby lamb

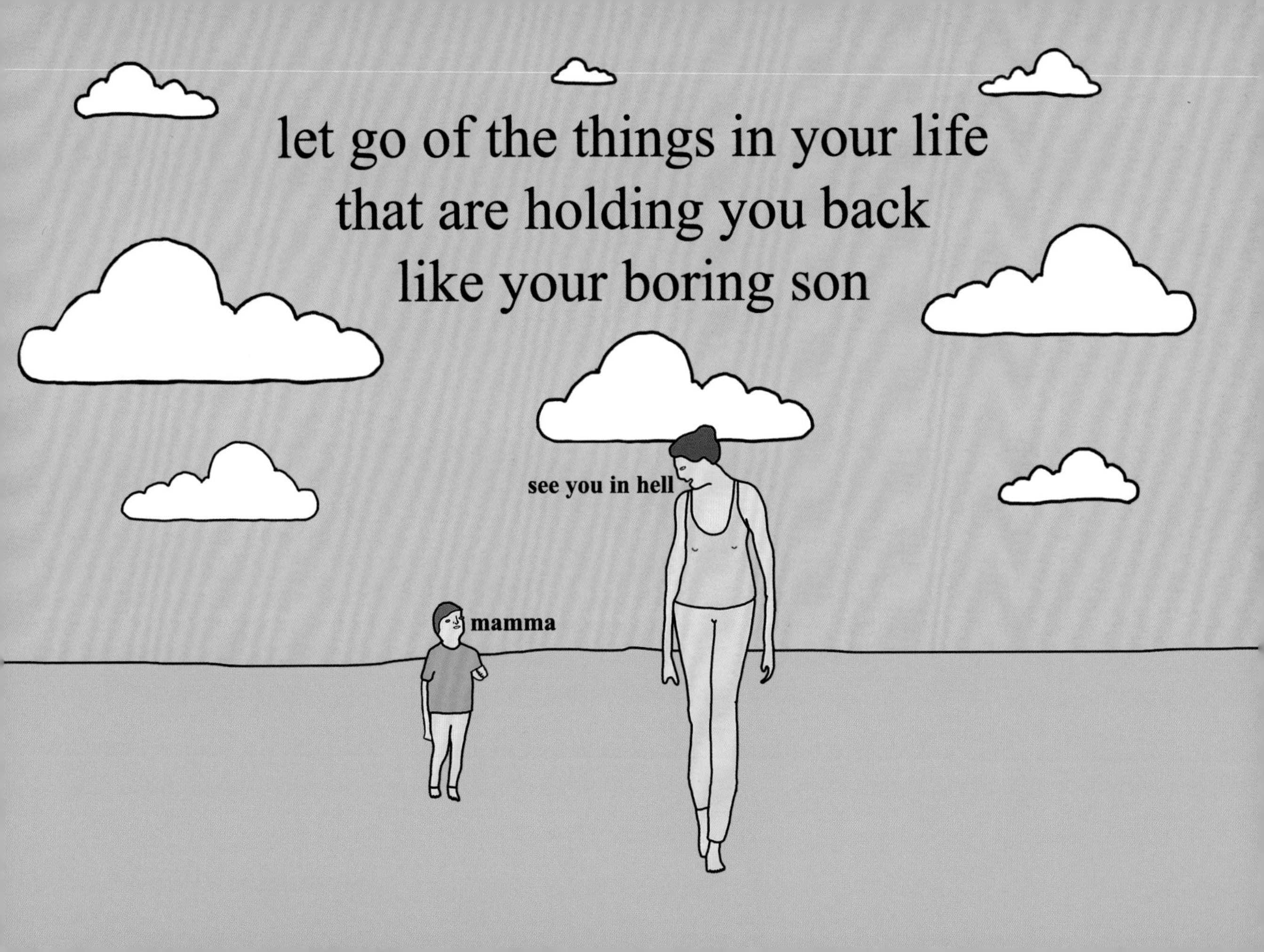
let go of the things in your life
that are holding you back
like your boring son
see you in hell
mamma

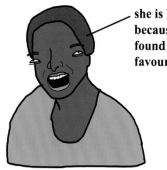

she is laughing
because she
found her
favourite cloth

he is laughing because
he saw a shoe shaped like
a little boy playing a
fiddle on top of a hill

# laugh more

she is laughing because
she loves looking
at pictures of pinecones
on her computer

he is laughing because
he has such tiny ears

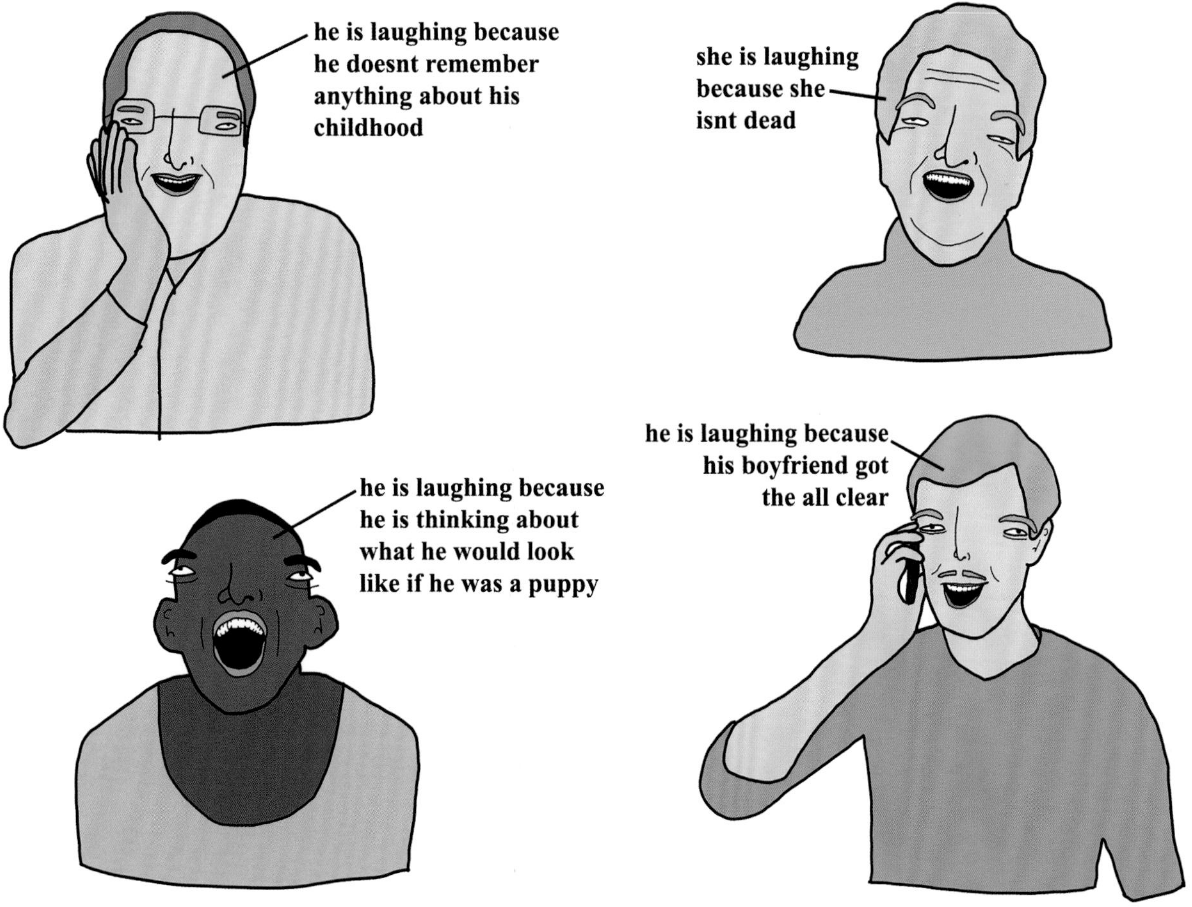
he is laughing because he doesnt remember anything about his childhood
she is laughing because she isnt dead
he is laughing because he is thinking about what he would look like if he was a puppy
he is laughing because his boyfriend got the all clear

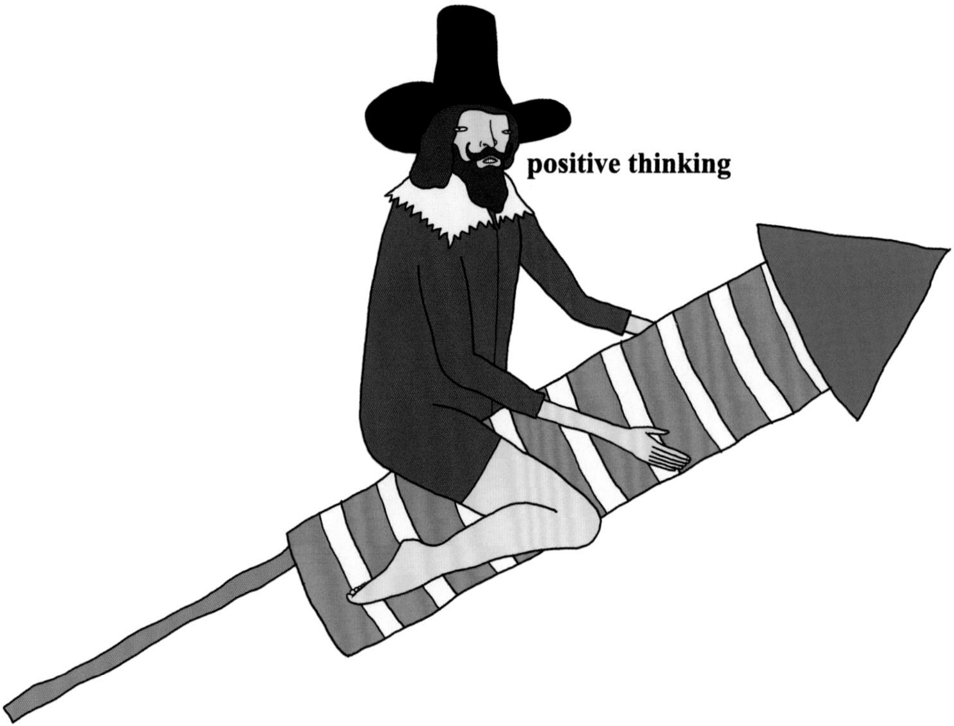
positive thinking

life is a massive firework
so sit on it and aim it for the stars

this little baby
who is so tiny and small
is going to make the biggest
and most massive difference
to the world of anyone of all

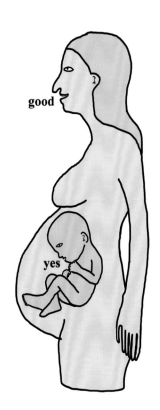

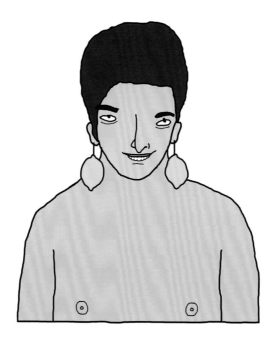

when life gives you lemons
make some lemon earrings

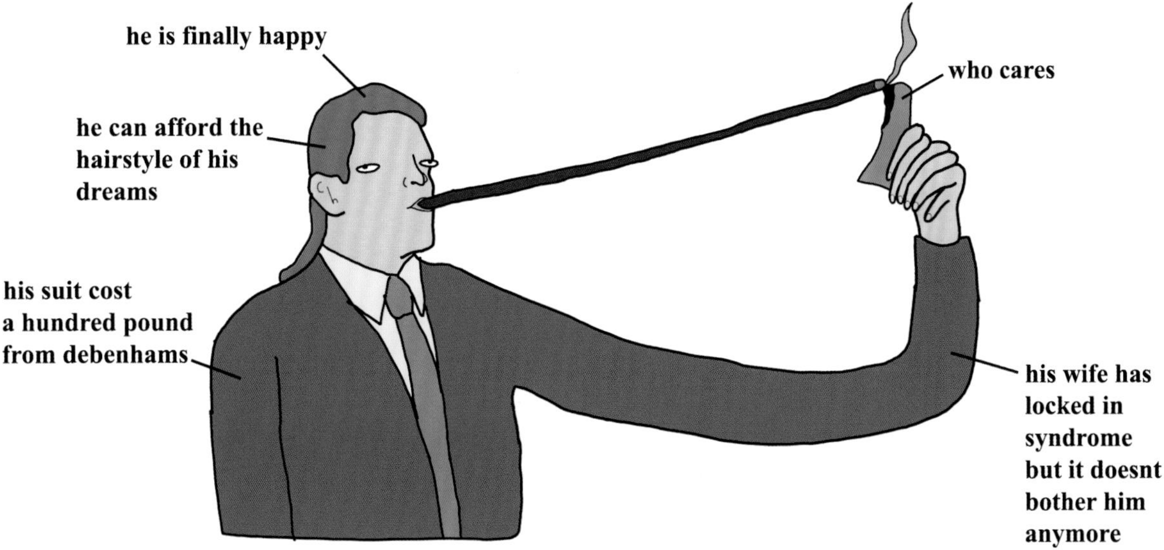
he is finally happy
he can afford the hairstyle of his dreams
his suit cost a hundred pound from debenhams
who cares
his wife has locked in syndrome but it doesnt bother him anymore

maybe you will win the lottery
and you will get loads of money
and everything will be ok again

i think it is
papas leg

what is
this bit

find out who
i truly am

let your family explore your body

# be more positive

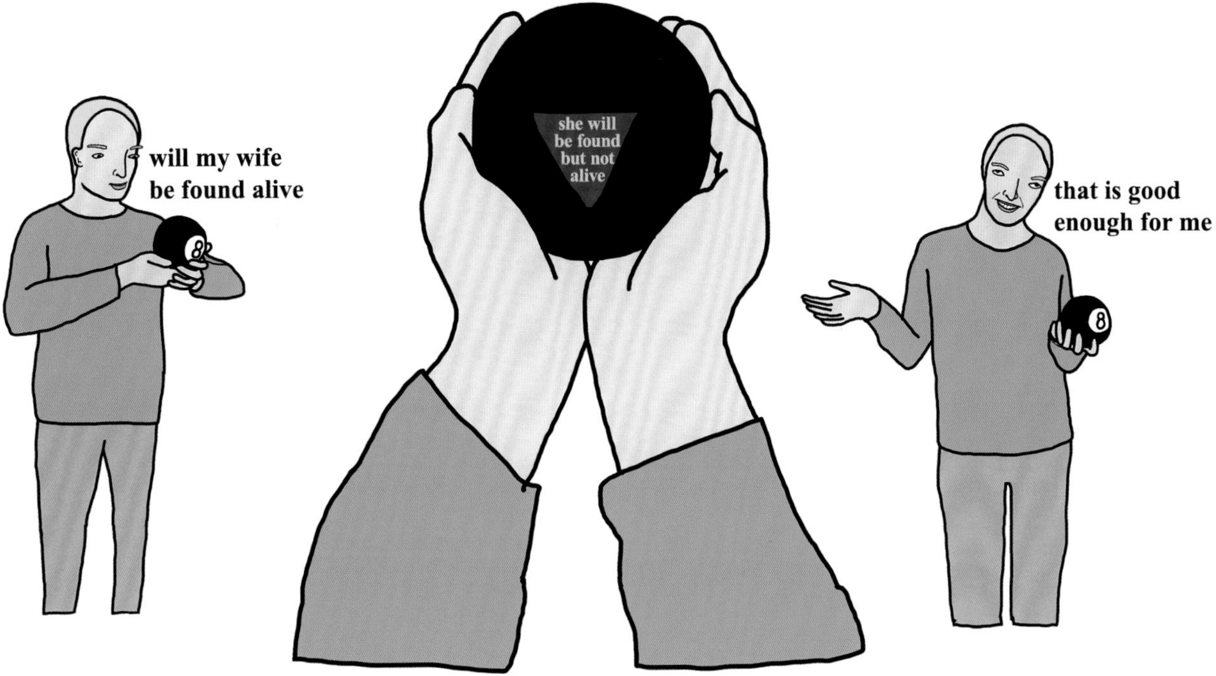
will my wife
be found alive
she will
be found
but not
alive
that is good
enough for me

# life begins
# at fifty

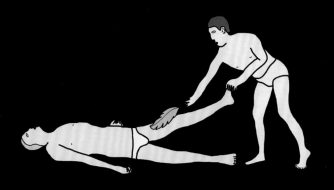

no feeling on all of the earth
is as true as the feeling of a man
tickling another mans legs
in complete darkness

it is more important for children to look up to the silver stars in the sky
and wonder about all of the beautiful things in the universe
than it is to look up to a star in a magazine and wonder where
they got their silver crop top from

if he feels stressed he just goes outside
and he milks his hen and then he feels
back to normal again

hens milk tastes
like wet eggs
it is delicious

milking a hen is a good way to relieve stress

love
can
be
found
in
the
most
strangest
of
places

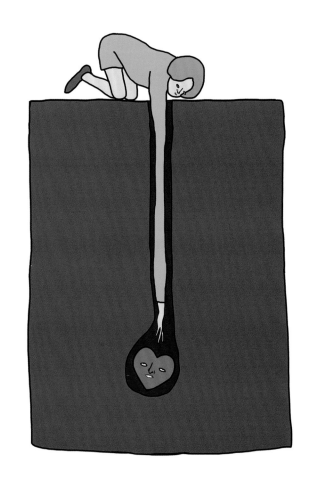

# make one wish every day

he wishes he didnt
have to wear a nappy
to his wifes christning

because today just might be the day that it comes true

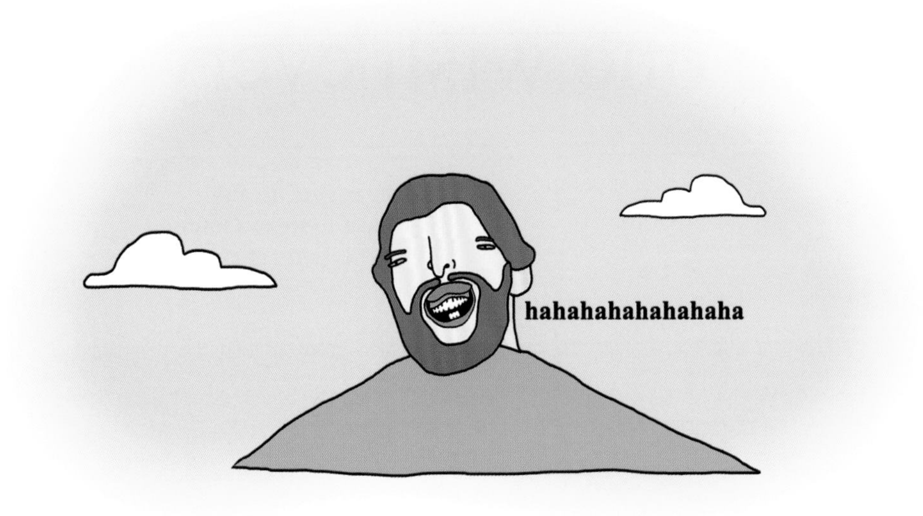
hahahahahahahaha

a hill is a perfect place
for you to rest your head

so what if you have nits

they are just hair pets

a man who doesnt love pancakes
is a man who has completely
given up on life

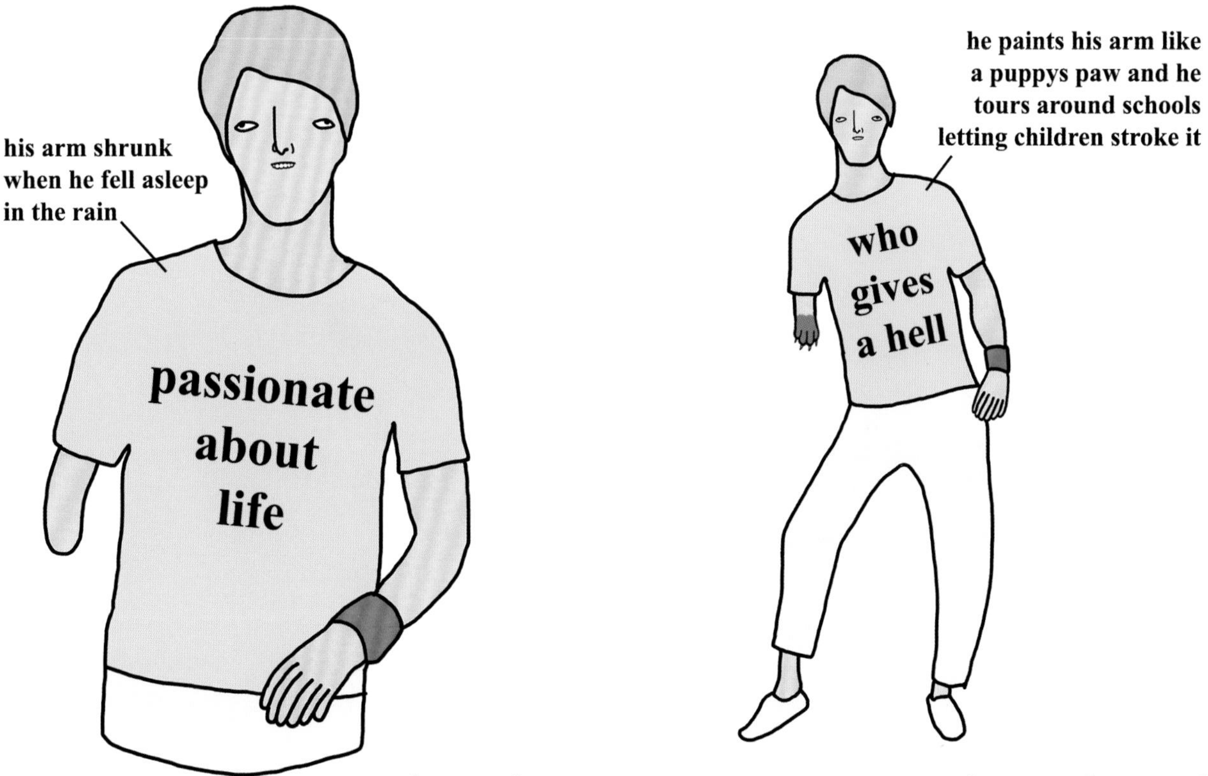
his arm shrunk
when he fell asleep
in the rain
passionate
about
life
he paints his arm like
a puppys paw and he
tours around schools
letting children stroke it
who
gives
a hell

just because your arm has shrunk
it doesnt mean your heart has to shrink as well

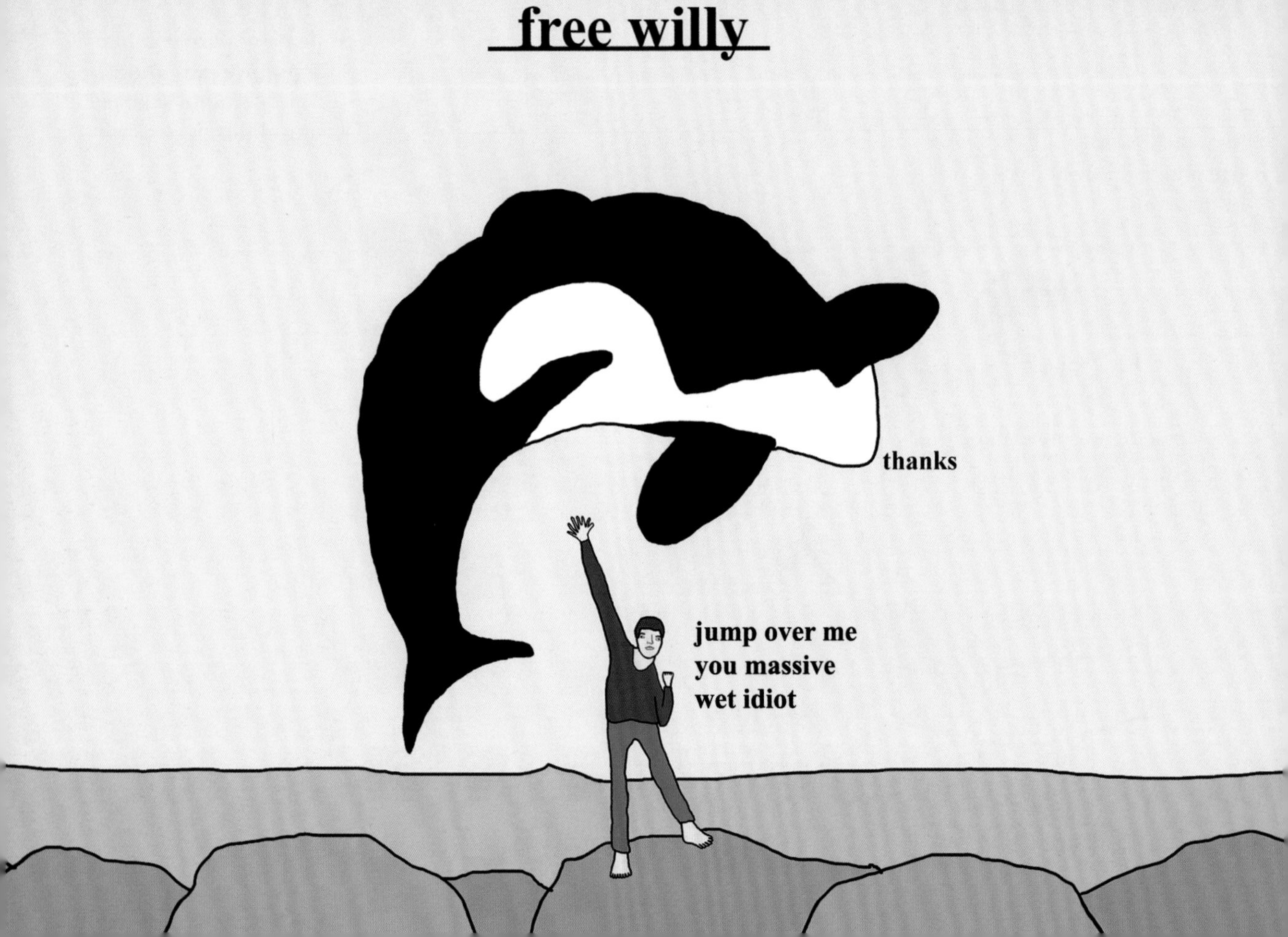
free willy
thanks
jump over me
you massive
wet idiot

is it a bird or is it a plane no it is a massive black dolphin jumping over a little boy that is right it is the film that is called free willy. if you havent seen free willy before then i feel really sorry for you because you are missing out on the greatest love story ever told about a little boy called jesse who falls in love with a massive black dolphin called free willy and my best bit in the whole of the film is when jesse is lay next to the swimming pool sun bathing and he is watching free willy just floating around like a big wet slug and jesse says to him what is wrong big guy but free willy just looks at jesse all sad and he doesnt say anything and jesse says that it is getting late and he has got to go back to his house because his mum will be wondering where he is again so he rollerblades back to his house and when he is sleeping at night time free willy slithers into jesses bedroom and he whispers to jesse if you love me then you will help me escape from the swimming pool and jesse cant believe that free willy can talk and free willy says yeah well it is hard to talk under water dont you know haha and he does a massive deep laugh and then him and jesse just look at each other for about 20 seconds and then free willy leans over jesse and he kisses him on his lips and it is so romantic and jesse says ok honey i will help you escape so the next morning jesse steals his mums gun and he takes it to the swimming pool where free willy is being kept and he shoots the lock on the main door of the swimming pool and loads of water goes everywhere and free willy manages to climb over a metal fence but there is loads of rocks in front of the sea and free willy screams damn it i knew it i ruddy knew it and jesse looks at free willy and he says you know what you have got to do and free willy nods and he says i know honey but i dont want to leave you and jesse says if you love me then you will be free because that is all i want you to be so free willy takes a massive run up and then he leaps out of the water and into the air and over his true love and as he splashes down into the sea his floppy weak fin goes completely stiff and healthy again and jesse screams thats my willy thats my willy thats my willy willy willy and then there is a slow motion close up of jesse picking up a dead fish from off the ground and kissing it and then the film just ends really suddenly and i think that to risk your own life for the person who you truly love is what true love is all about no matter who you may be even if you are a little boy or a massive black dolphin.

i hope emily and the children will forgive me for being so old

if you are really old then why not tie a cat or small goat around your face with some wire to make your family like you again

One day we will meet again
and on that day our smiles will
stretch for as far and wide
as the distance that we were apart

# put your thumb up if

he is putting his thumb up
because a girl in his class
let him borrow a pencil

he is putting his thumb up
because he hasnt been sick
all over himself today

# you are feeling confident

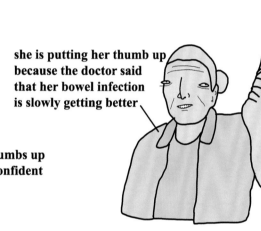

she is putting her thumb up because the doctor said that her bowel infection is slowly getting better

he is putting all of his thumbs up because he is singing a confident rhyme about a mouse inside of his head

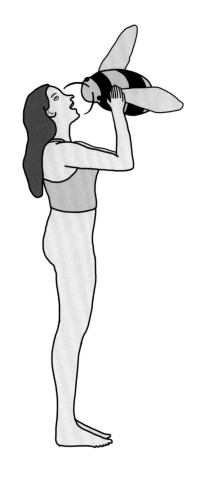

who cares
if your son is a bee

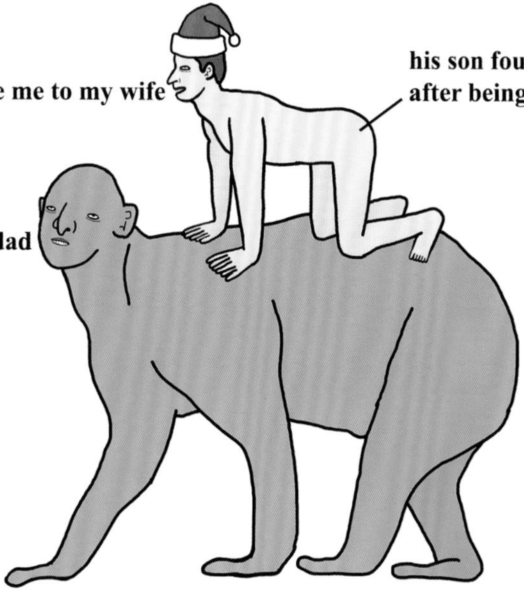
take me to my wife
his son found him in the woods
after being lost for nearly a year
merry christmas dad

the most important gift of all
is spending christmas with your family

let me taste your leg

harder

your precious gentle leg

precious leg

the most precious leg that i have
tasted in 465 years

why must
things be
this way

if you dont like the way your life is
then why dont you do something about it
instead of kneeling down with no clothes on all day

sucking up quiche out of a bumbag through a glass pipe will definetly give you the motivational boost that you have been searching for all of these years

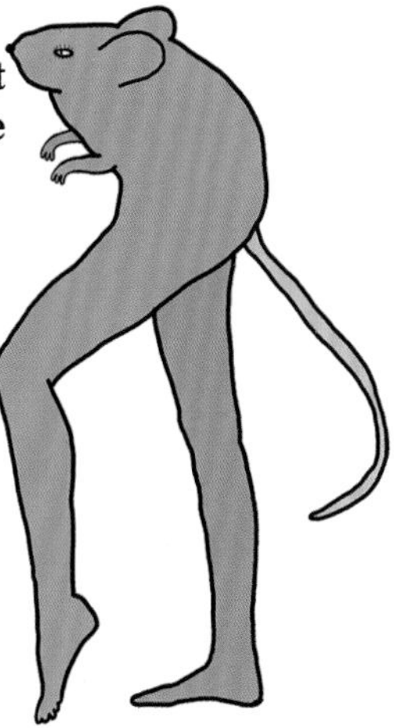
be as quiet
as a mouse

be quiet for a moment and you will see
such beautiful things around you and me

he stole a little boys school bag and he ate it in the woods
shh
he is worried that his wife will find out about what he did and make him have a divorce from her again
he saw the little boy walking to school the other day and he winked at him

people dont have to find out about your secret
that you have been hiding for the past year and a half
so stop worrying about it constantly

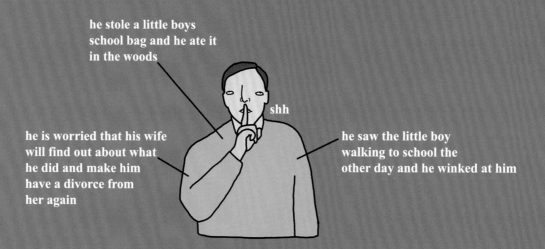

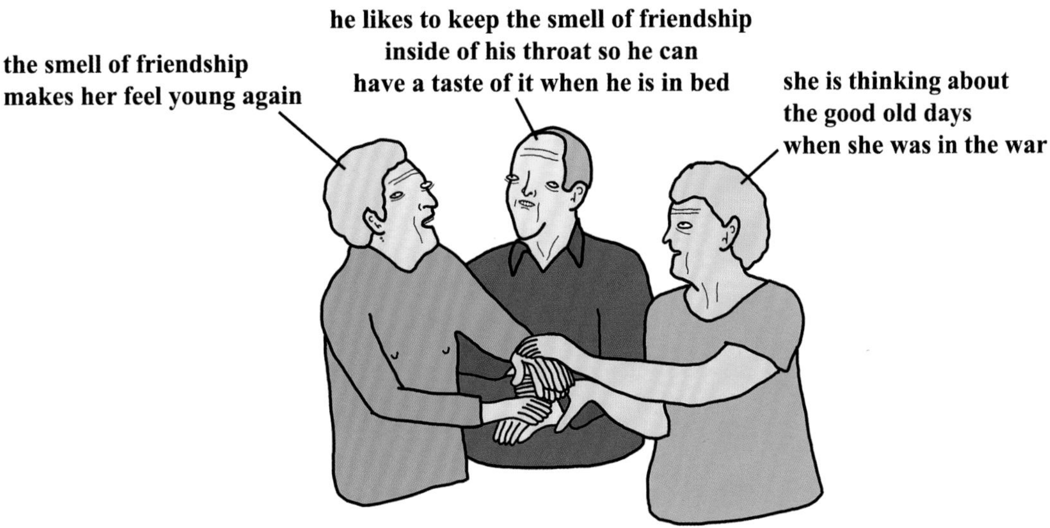
the smell of friendship
makes her feel young again
he likes to keep the smell of friendship
inside of his throat so he can
have a taste of it when he is in bed
she is thinking about
the good old days
when she was in the war

the soothing smell of friendship
is the only thing that you truly need

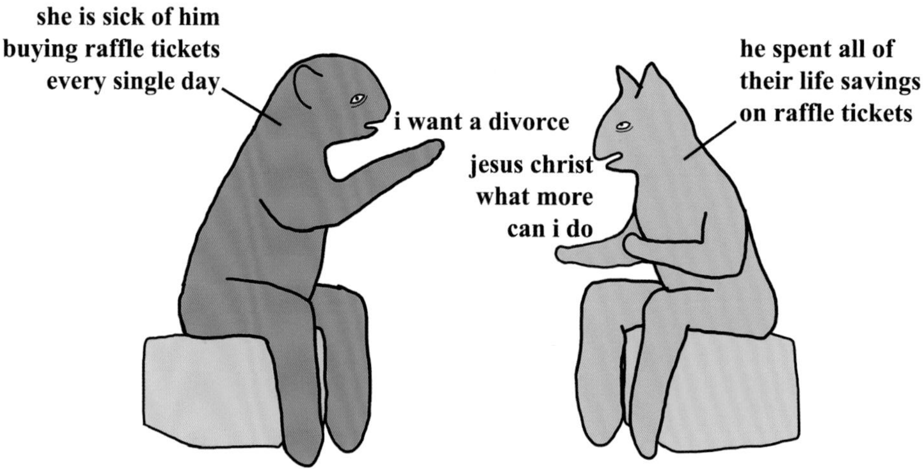
she is sick of him
buying raffle tickets
every single day
i want a divorce
jesus christ
what more
can i do
he spent all of
their life savings
on raffle tickets

some people dont deserve you in their life at all
so just say to them get out of my life and never come back
i have had enough of you

# twin sisters

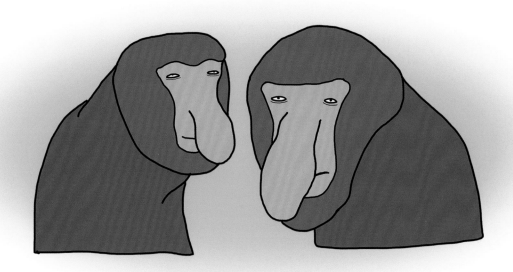

together forever and never apart
i will love you forever
inside of my heart

**i am the lord of the rings**

he is thirsty for rings of all shapes and sizes and his bum bag is filled with secret surprises that is right it is sonic the hedgehog the blue haired squirrel from the 3d family adventure game that is called sonic the hedgehog and the deaf prince of egypt. if you like the type of games that are about jewellery and bum bags then prepare yourself to go on a bum bag filled adventure of a lifetime and right at the start of the game it shows sonic the hedgehog standing behind his school with some boys from his class and he keeps on looking at his bum bag and smiling at it and all of the boys think that he is actually in love with his bum bag or something and then after about 5 minutes sonic slowly unzips his bum bag and it is filled right to the top with loads of quiche and he says to the boys do you think i can suck up all of this quiche out of my bum bag through this glass tube and they all look at sonic and they say do it if you want to do it mate but we are honestly not bothered if you do it or not and sonic says well i can do it so easy without even trying and his friend scott says fair enough sonyan if you want to do it then just do it but stop constantly going on about it to us every single day because it is just getting annoying now and then sonic says haha well read it and weep you bunch of cloth helmets and then he kneels down on the ground and he puts the glass tube over the quiche and he starts sucking it up out of his bum bag and all of the boys are just looking at each other and saying what is the actual point of him doing this and sonic was sucking it up so hard that he actually looked like he was having a quiche fit because his whole body was shaking so much and then once he had swallowed up every last taste from out of his bum bag he stands up and he says now that is how you unleash the quiche and a boy who is called jamie says well done sonic you just sucked up a massive slab of your mums quiche from out of your bum bag congratulations you must feel so proud of yourself and sonic says yes i do feel proud actually it is more than any of you idiots have done today and then sonic looks at his wrist and he says oh would you look at that it is time for me to go and collect some delicious golden rings haha and then he runs off over a hill and after about 2 minutes the boys get a text on their phones from sonic and it is a picture of him pretending to be crying and he is wiping his tears away with loads of gold rings and then on the last level of the game sonic the hedgehog has to battle the deaf prince of egypt who is played by teen throbsticle zac efron from the the film grease and sonic must defeat him or the world will be destroyed and turned into a paste and with every kick and slap to zac efrons deaf egyptian face a golden ring falls from the sky and then as quickly as a blink of a dolphins eye sonic jumps up into the air and he screams see you in hell zac efron and then he turns his legs turn into electric whisks and he slams them right into the side of zac efrons neck and his neck completely bursts open and the whole of the sky starts raining pure liquid gold like a beautiful golden shower falling right out of gods throat and then when the world has been saved and sonic has buried zac efron underneath his castle there is a shot of sonic standing on top of a mountain looking out over emerald city and he is smiling to himself and then he does a massive slow motion scream and loads of golden rings and quiche come flying out of his mouth and all of the villagers bellow eat the quiche and they spend the golden rings on new clothes and ipads and they all live happily ever after until the end of time.

dont be sad that it is sunday
just be happy that you arent dead

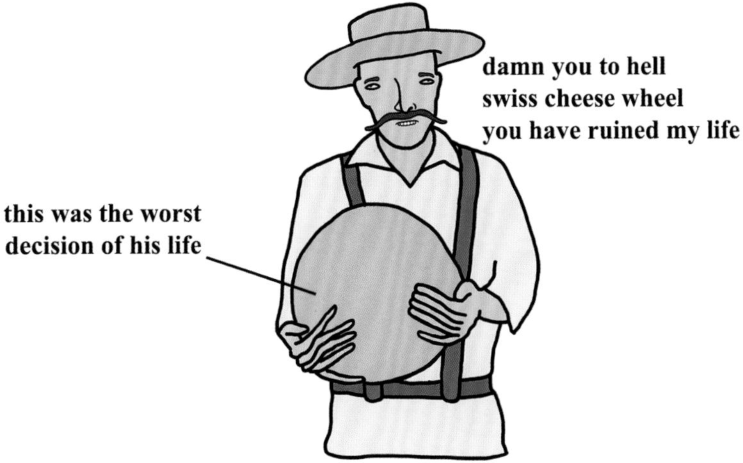
damn you to hell
swiss cheese wheel
you have ruined my life
this was the worst
decision of his life

# even the inventor of the swiss cheese wheel gets depressed sometimes

his dad bought him
a couple of internets for a
joke when he was 15 but
who is laughing now dad

he didnt know
what was real life
anymore

his family tried to put
him in a home but there
wasnt any internet there
so he escaped when it was
at night by digging a hole
in the wall with a dongle

online

now look at him

rest in paste

do you want to
end up like this

spend less time on your computer or you will
turn into some sort of internet paste and your
family will have to bury you inside a plastic tube

# you are what you eat

you

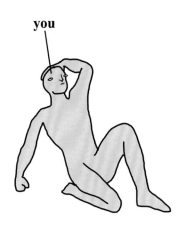

you in a month

what is wrong
i wish that i was dead

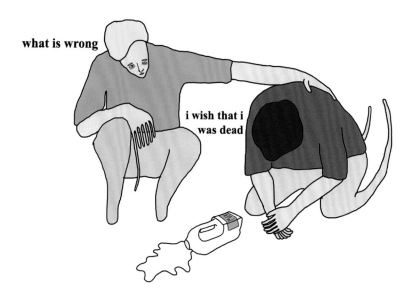

dont cry over spilt cow juice

the most sensitive part of your body
is the meat on the bottom of your feet

she is a lot more happier
since she started doing this
instead of going to her work
at the helmet factory

hold a little candle for
a extra slice of spice

maybe life isnt so
bad after all is it

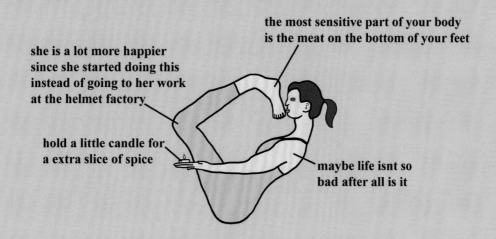

spoil yourself once in a while
because you deserve it

stop
worrying
so much

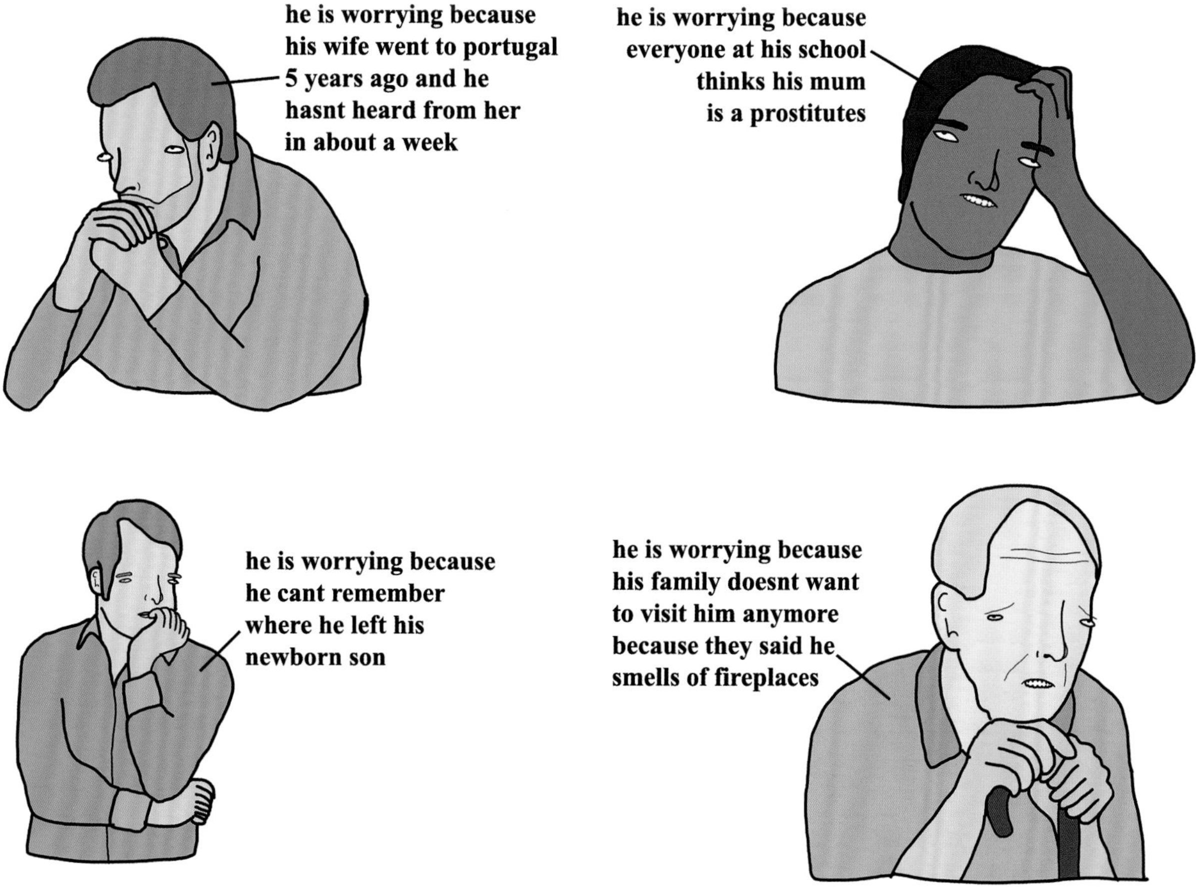
he is worrying because his wife went to portugal 5 years ago and he hasnt heard from her in about a week
he is worrying because everyone at his school thinks his mum is a prostitutes
he is worrying because he cant remember where he left his newborn son
he is worrying because his family doesnt want to visit him anymore because they said he smells of fireplaces

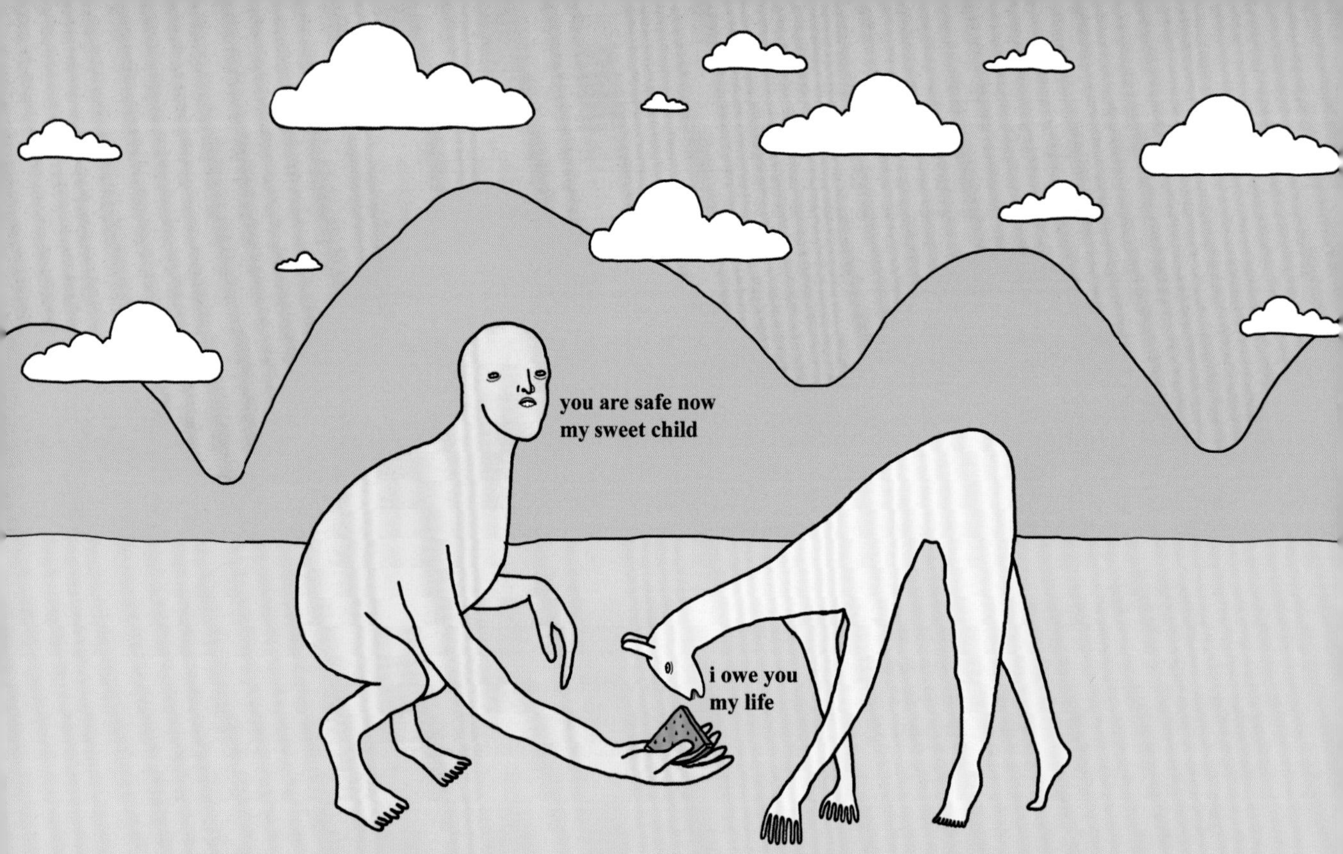
you are safe now
my sweet child
i owe you
my life

a friend is a person who will always be there for you when you really need them to be

this could be you

if you can actually be bothered getting out of your bed

and floating around the sky for a whole day

# the inside of a brain

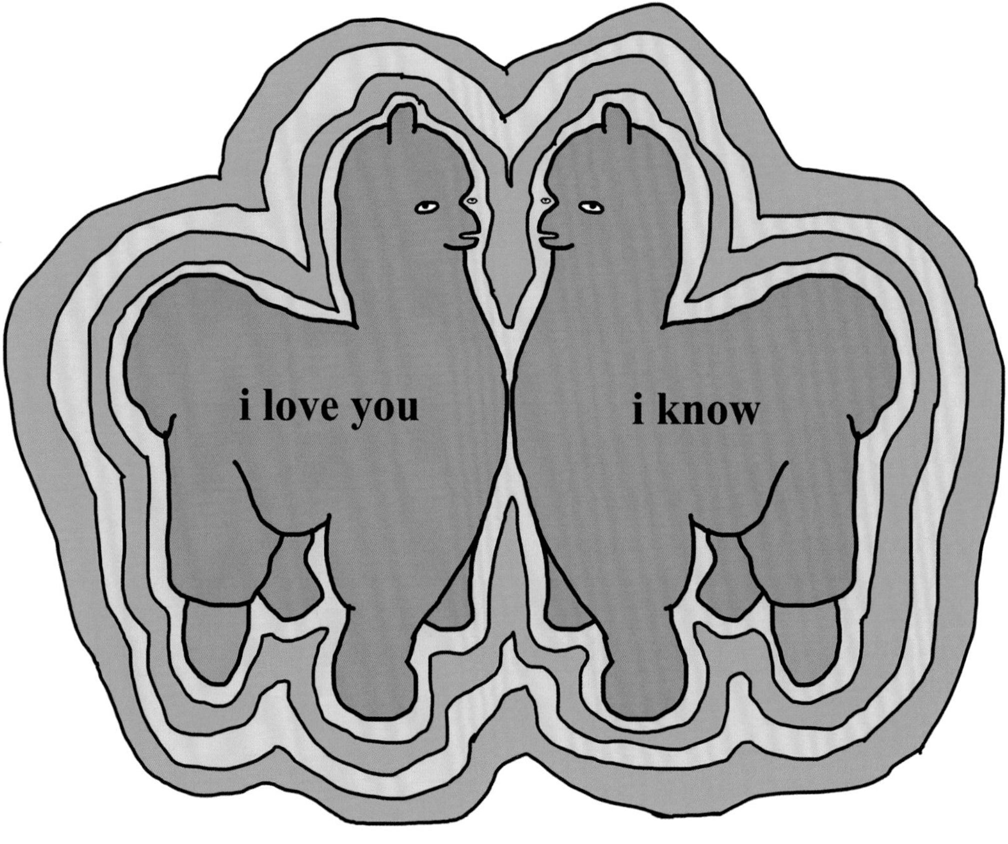
i love you
i know

dont ask her
about it

he just lies there
every single night
frightened to move
and terrified to ask

sometimes the less you know about your wife
the better your life will be

why was i
born a train

them things and at the start of the film it shows thomas the tank engine being born in a thunder and lightning storm and his dad who is the fat controller and his mum who is the main woman train at the train station are really frightened because they were told to never have a baby together and the fat controller even swore on his mums life when he took the job that he would never get any of the trains pregnant not even one of the small unused ones that they keep around the back and the train elders said to him that if he ever gets any of the trains pregnant then his first son will be born cursed with the body of a train and the legs and arms of a man and the fat controller said you got it there will be no pregnant trains around here haha trust me but then along came thomas and my best bit in the whole of the film is when thomas the tank engine

it is everyones favourite childrens film about a man who is trapped inside the body of a steam train that is right it is thomas the tank engine from the hit family film that is called thomas

the tank engine and the curse of fat controller. if you like films that are about curses and trains then prepare yourself to go on a train journey of a lifetime because it is about both of

is a teenager and he is fed up because he hates being a trains gender teen because he is really sensitive about his massive long mens beige legs and all of the other trains make fun of him and they call him thomas the rank engine and they spit on him all of the time as well and it makes him feel really fed up and then one day his friend henry says to him thomas have you ever thought about trying out for the local gymnastics team because you would probably be quite good at it and thomas said yeah right who would want me on their gymnastics team i am a freak and then henry says oh go on just give it a go there is no harm in trying and thomas says fine i will try out for the local gymnastics team because anything is better than being spat on all day here by these bunch of idiots so thomas goes to the village hall where the gymnastics team practice and he crawls in through the door covered in spit and he says i would like to join your gymnastics team and the gymnastics teacher walks over to thomas and she takes one look at him and she says you want to join my gymnastics team and thomas says yes and she says but you are a train and thomas says i know i am a train but i have got the heart of a man and she taps her bottom lip with her pen 3 times and then she nods her head and she says ok then lets see what ya got kiddo and then she points to a boy who has got a ghetto blaster on top of his head and he puts on the number 1 gymnastics song of the year that is called lucky boy by the daft punk experience and thomas the tank engine goes into the middle of the room and then he slowly stands up on to his hind legs and everyone cant believe how massive he actually is and everyone was saying that he was nearly about as big as a train and then thomas says here goes nothing and then he jumps up into the air and he does a massive sideways gymnastic spin and he blows loads of glitter out of his head chimney and everyone starts cheering and shouting come on and as he stood there in the middle of the room under the blanket of glitter slapping his massive long mens beige legs together in time to the music he finally felt free for the first time in his life because he had found a place where people accepted him for who he truly was and then right at the end of the film there is a shot of thomas the tank engine standing on top of a hill and he screams freedom in a really deep voice and then he stabs a massive sword into the ground in slow motion and then the film just ends really suddenly and it gave me such a fright.

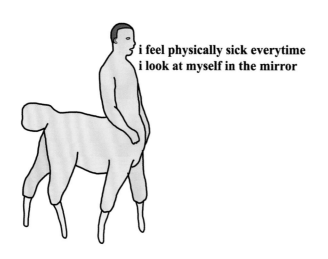

i feel physically sick everytime
i look at myself in the mirror

you cant even tell
you look fine

talking to someone
about your problems
can instantly make you feel better

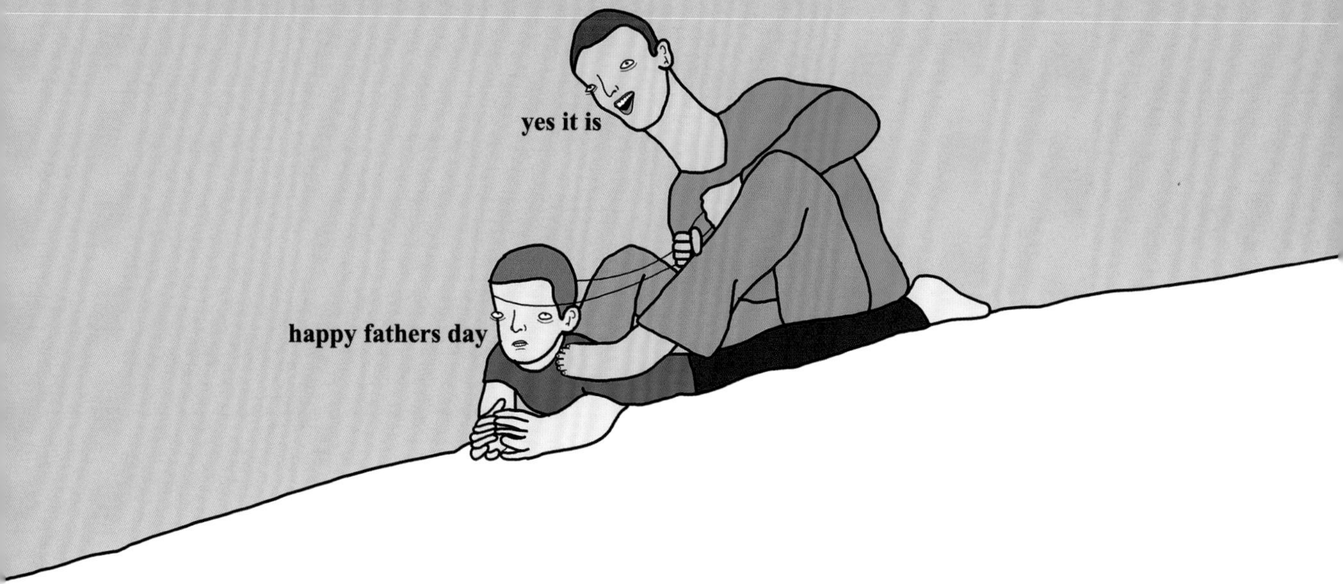
yes it is
happy fathers day

sometimes dads need
to have a bit of fun too

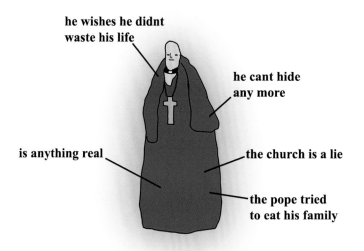

he wishes he didnt
waste his life

he cant hide
any more

is anything real

the church is a lie

the pope tried
to eat his family

# wish until it hurts

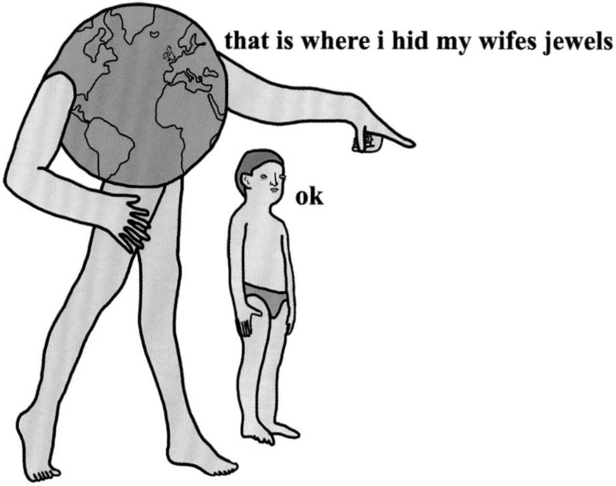
that is where i hid my wifes jewels
ok

open your heart

and let the world

show you all of its secrets

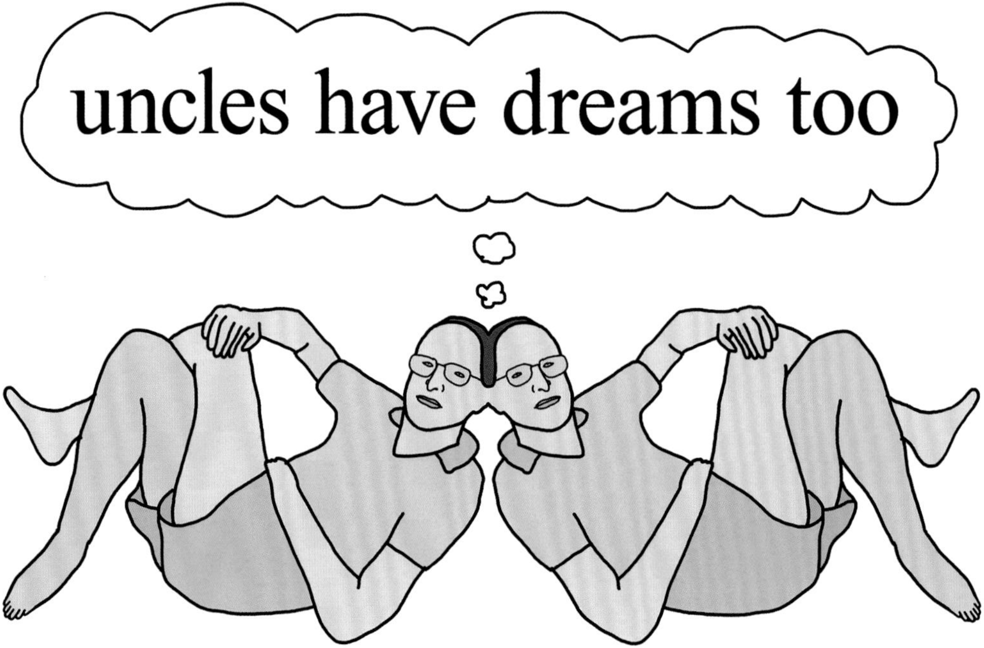
uncles have dreams too

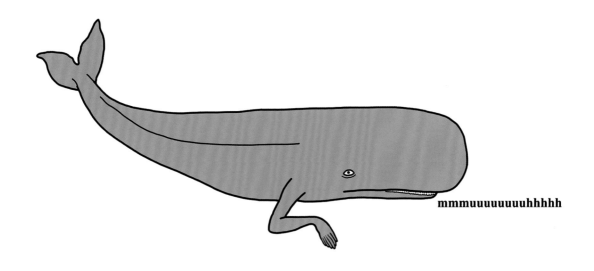

mmmuuuuuuuuhhhhh

there is nothing more beautiful than the
relaxing sound of a whales song

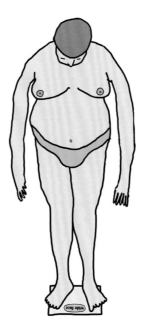

you are not fat
you just have a really wide face

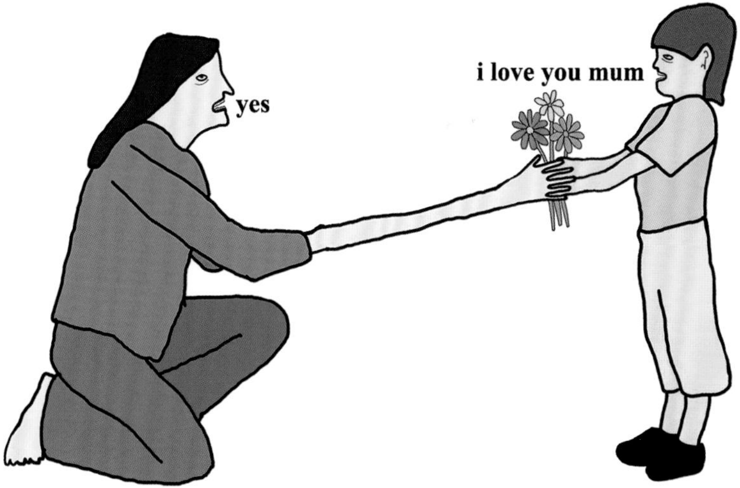
yes
i love you mum

mums are the creatures that hold the world together and if it wasnt for your mum then you probably would have never even been born

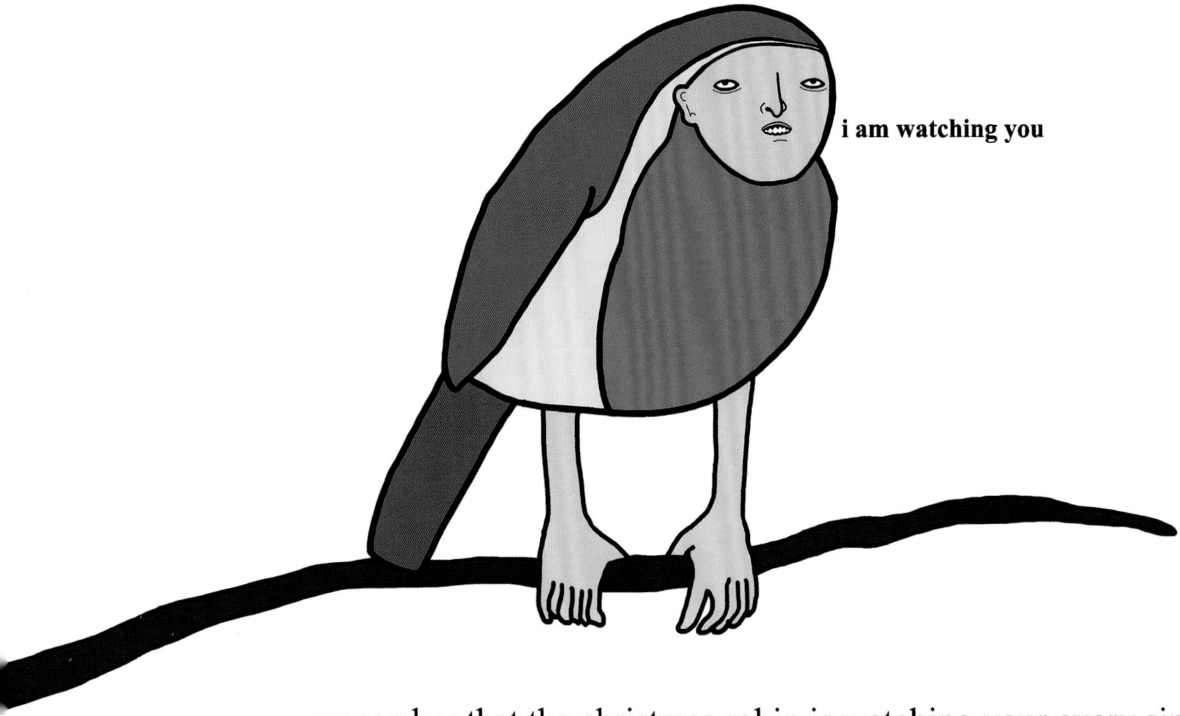
i am watching you

remember that the christmas robin is watching your every single move right now so make sure you are being good or else santa wont be climbing through your letterbox this year

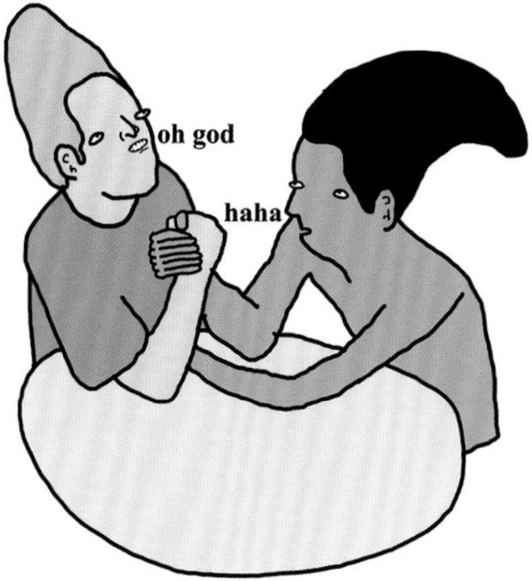
oh god
haha

if you cant beat them

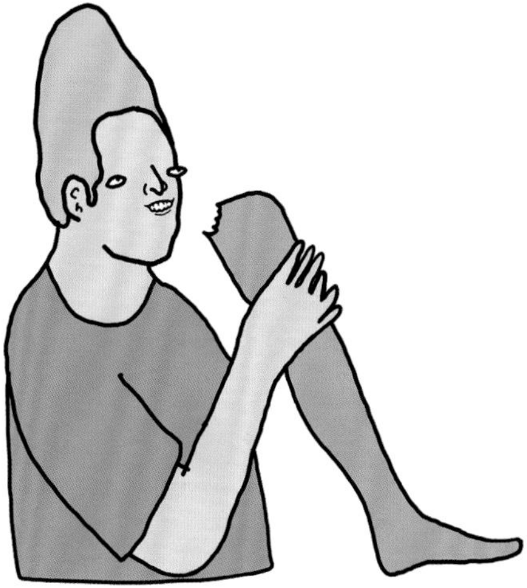

just eat them

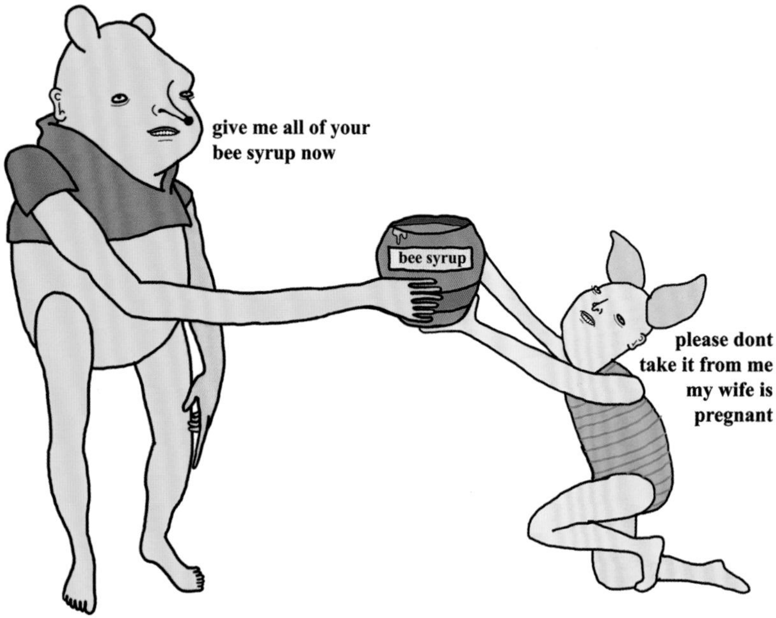
give me all of your bee syrup now
bee syrup
please dont take it from me my wife is pregnant

it is everyones favourite film about a syrup addicted bear that is right it is winnie the poo and his cousin piglet from the hit family film that is called winnie the poo and the chamber of syrup. if you havent seen winnie the poo and the chamber of syrup before then you might as well just be blind or deaf or both because you are missing out on a action packed adventure that will haunt you for the rest of your life and my best bit in the whole of the film is when winnie the poo is standing outside of his college in his red coloured crop top with his traditional no trousers on and he is making loads of people laugh by sucking syrup off the top of a teachers car and then gargling with it to the theme tune of mtvs sweet sixteen and all of his friends was saying that it was so funny and his friend ross even said that it was probably one of the best things that he has seen in about half a year and then tigger who is the main idiot at the college was going around telling everyone that he is going to punch winnie the poo in the back of his head after college when he is not looking because he hates him so much but it was so obvious that he is just jealous of winnie the poo for getting all of the attention from everyone and then after college tigger goes to punch him but winnie the poo senses his presence and he instantly turns around and slices tiggers spine with a bit of plastic that he found next to a fence and then winnie the poo goes on top of tigger on the ground and he does a massive screaming laugh right in tiggers face that sounded like a train full of bees smashing into a school and then before tigger could even say why cant i move my legs winnie the poo had completely vanished and then when it was at night time winnie the poo goes over to piglets house and he says for piglet to give him all of the syrup that he has got and piglet says you cant have it because my wife is pregnant and it is all that she can eat right now and winnie the poo says pregnant shmegnant i dont give a flying hell if she is pregnant or if she is just fat i just want to have all of your delicious golden bee juice inside of myself and then he slowly walks over to piglet and he kisses him on his forehead and he says my sweet cousin in a really light voice and then he looks at him for about 5 seconds and he does a half smile and then he slaps him right across his face and he bends forward and he licks piglets face where he was just slapped and he says give me your bee syrup now you salmon coloured dwarf and piglet says you need help mate you have got a serious syrup problem and winnie the poo says shut up no i do not and piglet says eh you do realise the reason everyone calls you winnie the poo is because you actually stink of poo because you never wash because all that you do is drink bee syrup all day and tigger said he actually saw you eating your own poo out of a napkin in the college car park as well and then winnie the poo just grabs the jar of syrup out of piglets pale pink palms and he runs out of the house and as he is running away he screams jumanji and then right at the end of the film there is a shot of winnie the poo sitting in the woods looking at a photograph of him and christopher robin in italy next to the eiffel tower and the camera goes really close up on winnie the poos face and he starts laughing and loads of bees fly out of his mouth and it lasts for about 5 minutes and then the screen just goes completely black and writing comes up that says winnie the poo hasnt been seen for nearly 2 and a half years and then a lightning bolt goes across the screen and it smashes the writing up into loads of little pieces and then the film just ends really suddenly and it really is one of the most action packed films that has ever been made about syrup and if you have children of your very own or if you can find a child just for a day then you should definitely have a watch of it with them when it is the summer holidays because trust me you will not regret it not even a slice.

if at first you dont succeed
give up and try something easier
or move abroad

he has been trying to
pull his head off for a
week now but he just
cant quite do it

his family keep telling
him there is no point
trying to pull his head
off because he will
never be able to do it

he saw a man
do it in a film

he says he is going to do it
even if he dies trying

he did it

it is fine to be curious about things
(turn to the next page if you are feeling curious today)

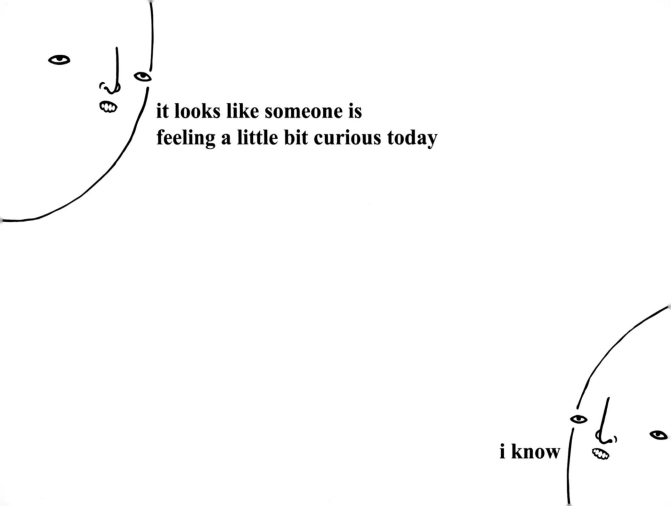

it looks like someone is
feeling a little bit curious today

i know

kiss this page
to make yourself
not feel so alone
anymore

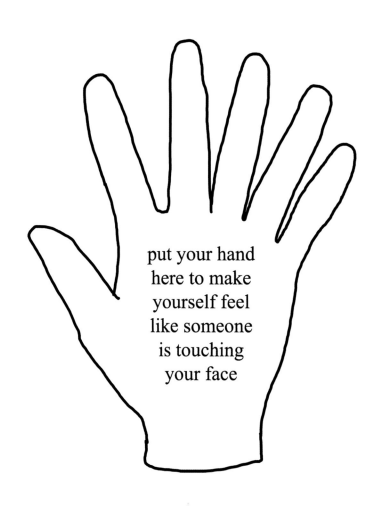

put your hand
here to make
yourself feel
like someone
is touching
your face

## outroduction

now that you have finished having a read of this book
i hope that it has made you feel more positive about yourself

and remember that whenever you may feel sad or a bit down about your life
then just pick up this book and hold it next to your face and let the
pictures and words stroke your whole body and tell you
that everything is going to be ok

because i believe in you
and you should do too.

love from your friend

chris (simpsons artist) xox

also by chris (simpsons artist)

# the story of life

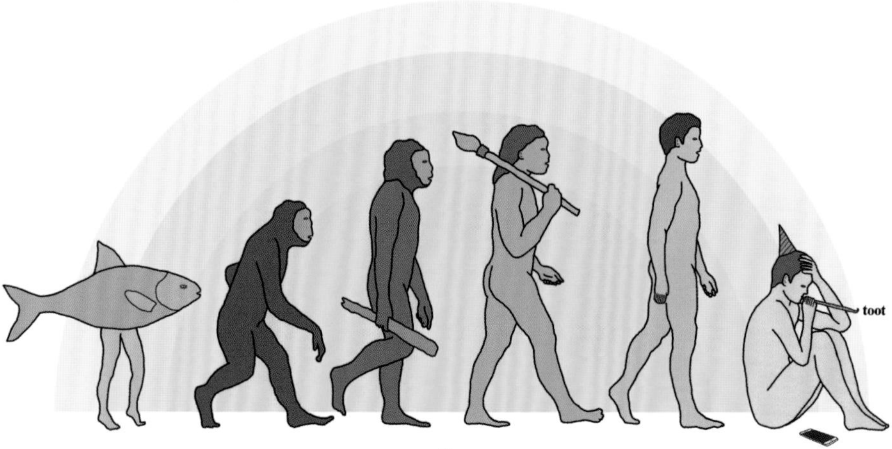
toot

by

chris (simpsons artist)

available now

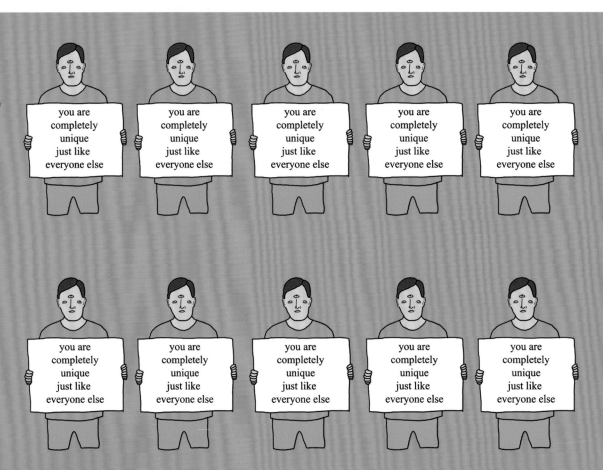

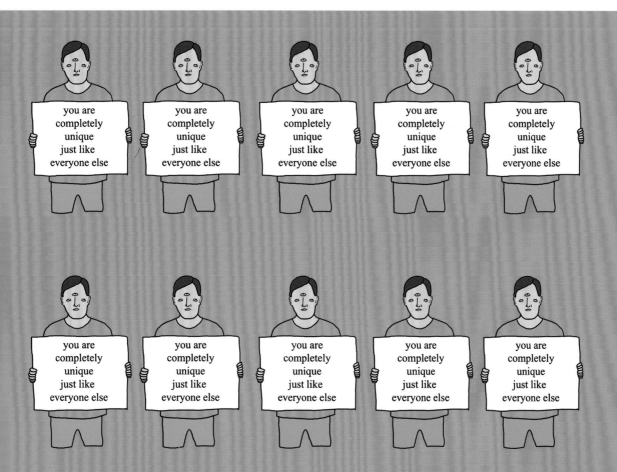

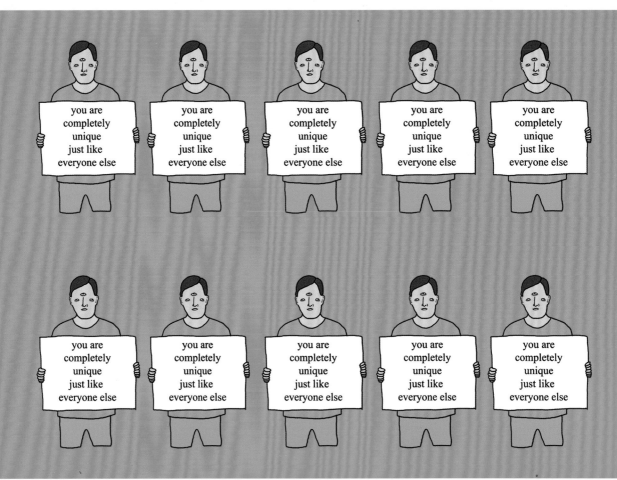